AMERICA

IT WAS JUST AN IDEA

BY

DR. RAYNA M. GANGI

ISBN 1537244949

CHAPTER 1

I was born in a country that was in between wars, a place where woodwork and homes were being painted white, an attempt at feeling whole and pure again after a devastating world war. Men were home helping to create babies and finding their way back into a workforce that was for a while mandated by war and dominated by women. My mother had worked in ammunition factories with friends who also lied about their ages and traveled away from home to help the war effort. My father was an Army Air Corps pilot with four brothers who also returned home to a country in transition.

My first few years were spent with babysitters and a grandmother so my parents could continue building a family business, and striving for the elusive American dream. I wasn't born angry, nor did I know the history of my nation, but I was raised to salute my flag, enjoy the parades down main street, respect and obey my teachers, never trespass, and to say the pledge of allegiance to a country who let me be born free.

The conflict in Korea would take my father to war again, and I would stay up waiting for him to come home, not knowing the concept of time or the meaning of war.

Televisions were making their way into every household, and the programs were simple, entertaining, filled with black hat bad guys and white hat heroes. It was only turned on at night, at least as far as the children knew, because days were filled with chores and play, often creative as toys were scarce, and often alone as friends were just as busy. If we wanted to play baseball or soccer or basketball, we rode our bikes or walked to the fields. Mothers were either working outside the home, or being homemakers, a full- time job that didn't allow for car rides to find creative play outlets, or to satisfy a child's notion of what should be important.

When my dad returned from Korea, the family restaurant business became a priority again, and as I and my siblings grew, we were expected to work as soon as we could, usually by ten years old, and we were proud and happy to finally reach the age where we could be included and working. We didn't make a lot of money, nor were we given an allowance that allowed anything more than saving it until we had enough to put in the bank, but we developed a work ethic that stayed with us, an ethic that told us to be on time, give it our all, be proud of our jobs, and be grateful we could contribute.

School was mandatory, and most of us knew what was expected of us. Grades were based on knowledge and effort, but also on potential, and I strove to show my potential and exceed whenever I could. My teachers were counselors and coaches, surrogate parents and disciplinarians, and we all knew that any misbehavior would not only mean a trip to the office, but also the dreaded note to mom or dad that said they needed to intervene and provide punishment. My parents were no different from any others and complied with that understanding. Because of that, most of us made sure we didn't get into any trouble and have to face the consequences.

Every morning we faced the flag and pledged our allegiance. We didn't understand that pledge when we were young, but as we learned about the world in social studies and current events, we began to, at the very least, feel our allegiance and duty to our country. And we loved it.

Church wasn't as high on the list as it was for many others because the restaurant was open on Sundays, but we did make sure to go on Easter and Christmas Eve, and those who weren't small business owners made up the congregation and understood why others weren't there. We never questioned why some kids went to a Catholic church and others to a Methodist, or why some kids went to a synagogue or a temple. Religion was personal and not judged, as long as that religion promoted good will, peace, and followed God. I didn't know or understand the differences in denominations until I was older, but I did know when someone had lost or forgotten God, because they were always on the wrong side of the law or humanity, always in trouble, and always avoided.

My grandfather had told me I would be known by the company I keep, and I didn't want to be known as the bad guy or outlaw.

Our curriculum through grammar school taught us to read and write, but more importantly, it taught us to think, be creative, and be open-minded about ideas. Music and art were as important as math and science, so by first grade, we all started flutophone, joined the choir or chorus, and maintained our physical fitness with recess and after school sports.

It wasn't until I was thirteen that I began to understand the importance of American politics and the current and past events that defined who I was as an American. I played John Kennedy in a mock debate, something my Republican parents weren't happy about, but my opponent got confused and starting using the Democrat talking points instead of Richard Nixon's platform. I knew both sides of the arguments and reveled in making my opponent cower to my words when he realized he was on the wrong side. I didn't agree with Kennedy's platform, but after that debate, I followed both political parties and listened intently to speeches.

When Kennedy was assassinated, I instinctively knew my life, the life of every American, would be changed forever. I watched Jackie and Caroline go to the casket and kneel, Teddy and Bobby accompany the hearse on the long walk, and John-John salute his father's riderless horse and flag. No one could tell me why he was shot or who did it. Lee Harvey Oswald was the alleged assassin, but somehow I knew there was more to the story. Because of my education, I was already fairly good at reading people, the body language and words they used. Something wasn't right. I waited impatiently for the Warren Report and read it over and over again once it arrived.

My parents and friends offered no help in understanding. They were busy with their work or friends and had no interest in a culture they said was corrupt. My grandmother did tell me that she felt FDR was the beginning of a political world that didn't serve the people. She said everyone was grateful for the WPA program, but the people didn't understand it was a program to make people feel indebted to the party, and that the war and recession were brought on by the same politicians who now wanted to be seen as heroes and saviors.

My older grandfather said it began with Woodrow Wilson and the first World War, that Democrats were always getting America into wars and then Republicans had to get us out. He said Viet Nam would be the same, that Kennedy might have avoided it, but that that conflict would be a full-blown war now that he was gone. He said, "Mark my words. Long after I'm gone, you'll find that Kennedy's murder was done by those who Americans trusted. Oswald said he was a patsy, and he was."

That was the first time I remember suddenly being angry at those who govern America. Older friends were already being drafted, and we too often had an assembly to honor the death of a fellow student, someone's son, someone's friend. I wasn't against the war, but I also wasn't for it. No one could say why we were involved, who we were fighting and how we would win. Our televisions were now filled with stories of the wounded, and the news programs became the center of the lives of many families. Each time I saw a report or read a headline, I could feel the anger that was now a part of me.

Baseball and soccer took on a new meaning. The joy of competition was becoming more personalized, as if losing was okay because at least we tried, and winning was because of some person and not because of a team. There was at the same time an anger in the coaches and parents that I hadn't seen before. It was okay if we lost, but not really. They were older and were more a part of a generation that knew how to win. The news stories told me we weren't winning in Viet Nam even though brave men and women were trying, so I looked at the coaches, the generals and Lyndon Johnson, and I knew it was because they didn't want to win, that the troops, the team on the field, would feel defeat and have to learn to live with it. My friends who did return from Viet Nam were forever changed, and many of my other friends decided to believe the news stories that now pervaded our lives, stories that said we were wrong to be there, wrong in how we fought this war, and it was the soldier or the Marine or the sailor who were now the black hat bad guys. I greeted those returning with pride, but so many others expressed only anger and disdain for those who heeded the call of our government and followed the lead of our President.

We were Americans, and our ancestors had taught us allegiance, right or wrong. The greatest country on earth wasn't perfect, but it was a young country that at least was trying to be free. I fought with those who spat on the returning warriors. It was the soldier who followed orders, the Marine who landed first, the sailor who brought the troops to shore, each signing their life away on enlistment, who allowed the rest of us to either demonstrate in the streets or honor the fallen. I was angry that so many didn't understand and had turned on friends in uniform, as if they were the ones who decided there was some financial gain or power in being in Viet Nam, in being in any war.

At the age of seventeen, I read the Constitution for the first time. Both the Declaration of Independence and the Constitution had been taught to us in school, but never the history behind those documents, never the details of what every word meant, or the sacred duty of every American to read them and understand the birth of our nation, the birth of the Republic. We learned about Franklin and Adams, Thomas Jefferson, George Washington, but the context of the freedom they provided was never clear.

Our parents knew. When Japan attacked Pearl Harbor there was no question that we had to fight back, even though we had maintained an isolationist ideology and avoided understanding Hitler's rise in Europe. Japan attacked our families, our home, and that ignited an anger that caused millions of men and women to join forces and defeat the other "team."

MacArthur and Patton and Eisenhower became the coaches who would lead America to victory, just as the three percent of

Americans under Washington had led us to victory over a tyrannical king. The president's job was to protect our borders, and every soldier took an oath to defend the constitution against all enemies, foreign or domestic.

I read these sacred documents and again felt my anger. Where did it say we should advise other countries or interfere in their politics? How were we protecting our borders from the North Vietnamese? Why was Johnson so intent on escalating what began as a conflict to a full- scale war? Why was Kennedy assassinated and who really was responsible?

I was almost eighteen, and I was an angry American.

CHAPTER 2

I turned eighteen, was distracted by Beatlemania as most were in my circles, and still too young to truly understand the world. Viet Nam was going strong in 1968, so like my brother before me, I enlisted in the Marines. It was a duty I believed in regardless of my stance on war. If my country was in a fight, I owed my time, my skills, and my life. There was only a slight chance I'd see combat, but if I did, I was ready and willing. For God and country became my mantra, and my quest was to write about the war so others could understand why we were there. I was sent to electronics school instead of journalism. Nixon was the President and Camp Pendleton was my base, a sad, almost frightening place where men were trained to fight, and to also prepare to die.

The televisions in the barracks were almost always tuned to the news, but most didn't want to know or didn't care. We heard taps every night, but we also heard taps throughout the day. We were losing and none of us knew why. We were supposed to be fighting Communism, but the leadership in Washington didn't seem to know how, or didn't truly want to win.

I researched Richard Nixon and as much of his inner circle that I could find. I wanted to know who was now keeping us in this war, or if he was the man who would lead us to victory so we could get out. I was surprised to find his connections to Johnson, to the CIA, to Kennedy and the big banks. My family members were Republicans, and though I would have voted for John Kennedy if I could, I was raised to think Republicans kept us out of war. Wilson had broken his promise to enter World War I, betrayed the country by starting the Federal Reserve. Johnson played a key role in the Kennedy assassination and his Great Society, the latest stage of progressivism that would enable a welfare state to ensure future Democrat voters. So why was a Republican president maintaining a war that was being lost?

I asked as many people as I could and didn't care if they were enlisted or officers. At one point, I was in a group of Marines who had just returned from Viet Nam, and in the course of the conversation, I overheard one say that weapons stored on base had been stolen.

"It's not the first time," he said. "And I know where those weapons are. They're being shipped to the Cong, the North Vietnamese."

I interrupted. "I don't believe that. Who would ship weapons to them?"

The sergeant glared at me. "Don't be naïve, Marine. We ain't nothin' but pawns for politicians. And the people in South Nam? They're going to get screwed."

"He's right," another added. "War is about profits, for the bankers, the brokers, the politicians. They play both sides just like they did in the big one."

"Doesn't make sense," I said. "Nixon is anti-Communist. He served under Eisenhower. Why would he want us to ose?" Not him!"

The sergeant was getting very angry and also very paranoid. He looked behind him and off into the distance before he continued. "Congress. Check out Congress and Agnew." He took a drag off a cigarette, blew the smoke in my face, and pointed his finger at me.

"I know who stole them weapons and I know why. You like to know things? Study the Communists in America. Check out where the Nazis came after World War II. And Agnew? He's got a history no one paid any attention to. He won't be around long."

Over the next few months, hundreds of friends were brought home to be buried. I watched the news more often so I could learn about Nixon, and I was encouraged that he spoke of ending the war, but my anger over the many deaths was constant, and I was learning to distrust what I heard on the news, and what I heard from my president.

The anti-war movement was gaining momentum, as was the black movement, drug usage, and demonstrations on every corner. Young Democrats were parading in the streets shouting anti-war slogans, but it was their votes who put Kennedy and Johnson in office. It was their votes that empowered the Kennedy assassins so Viet Nam would escalate to a war. The Beatles were writing songs about peace, and I was ready to end my enlistment to see the country and learn more about what it meant to be an American.

Nixon was re-elected in a landslide and he did attempt to end the war in 1973. He brought back many POWs, but also left many behind. He ended the draft and traveled to China. But America was still in trouble.

Many of my military friends refused to speak about their tours in Nam, but they did speak about their hatred for Jane Fonda, calling her, among many names, a traitor. They were angry. We were leaving the South Vietnamese as losers and the people would feel the wrath from the North without protection. Fonda was a Hollywood Democrat, a pro-Communist sympathizer, who traveled to North Viet Nam as an anti-war activist. She was given the title "Hanoi Jane," when she was photographed on a NVA anti-aircraft gun, a photo she said was incidental and possibly planned by the North Vietnamese as propaganda. I couldn't discern the truth. The hypocrisy of the Democrats fighting as antiwar activists when they were, in my mind, responsible for that war, was too overwhelming to get clear on anyone's true intentions.

Anti-war demonstrations did help to end the war, but not before students at Kent State were gunned down during a demonstration and not before more than 58,000 of our military were killed.

I believed that the American people could make a difference, that our Constitution gave us the right to demonstrate and that politicians would respond to those demonstrations even if their response was just to keep their positions. I held onto that belief as calls for Nixon's impeachment made it to petition lines in New York City after the Watergate break in and subsequent scandal.

Agnew was already gone, as my Marine friend had promised, only the second vice president to ever resign, and now Nixon was resigning with a peace sign as his legacy. It was the people who caused Nixon's resignation. It was the pressure of the people, and to me, that was a positive side to all the chaos in government, a positive result of being a Republic and having the freedoms the Constitution promised.

I was still angry, but a relatively placid Ford presidency allowed the country to regroup and recover from Viet Nam. Nixon had opened doors to China and started the Environmental

Protection Agency. Colleges were promoting women's equality, and computers were just beginning to become a household word. The world was still chaotic, POWs were still in Nam, veterans were still being spit on, but America, IBM, and the seventies allowed us all to dance a little crazy and forget about war for a while.

By 1977, we had another Democrat for President. The peanut farmer from Georgia, Jimmy Carter, was the fourth in a string of liberal progressives who would tax and spend, be weak in foreign affairs, give away the Panama Canal, and start two new agencies to grow government even more than his predecessors.

My grandfather was very upset when Carter won and voiced his opinion loudly at family parties.

"Carter is another Johnson, another Wilson, another liberal southerner."

"I heard he pardoned all the draft dodgers," I said.

"Yes, he did," Grandpa answered. "He'll pardon criminals, tax our electricity and give the country away while he's doing it."

"Wasn't FDR a Democrat?" I asked.

"Oh, yes. Good old FDR." He settled into his favorite chair which told me I was in for a history lesson. "A lot of people liked FDR, even though it was Eleanor who really ran the White House while he was out at Hot Springs with his mistress. FDR. The three term president. He got so many people dependent on the government that they believed he was the only answer for their survival."

"Like Johnson," I said.

"Johnson picked up where FDR left off. The Communist takeover of America has been going on since the Fabian Socialists arrived on our soil. George Bernard Shaw was a famous one. Your uncle saw him in Chicago, heard him say if you're old or sick or disabled, you have no business being alive. He's part of that whole bunch in Chicago and New York. And in Washington."

I had no idea who the Fabian Socialists were and I hoped he would explain, but he was tired and promptly dozed off.

Carter went to work every morning in cardigan sweaters, to me, a sign of weakness and a symbol that the White House was no longer a powerful office of a powerful country. I wasn't the only one who felt that way. Apparently, so did the Iranians.

I researched as much as I could about Iran, but it wasn't a prominent story or one news people wanted to cover. Iran was one of the most oil-rich countries in the world, but after a CIA led coup in 1953, Iranians began to resent American intervention in their affairs. Why wouldn't they? The new leader was a member of Iran's royal family named Mohammed Reza Shah Pahlavi. The Shah's government was secular, anti-communist, and pro-Western. In exchange for tens of millions of dollars in foreign aid, he returned 80 percent of Iran's oil reserves to the Americans and the British.

For the C.I.A. and oil interests, the 1953 coup was a success. In fact, it served as a model for other covert operations during the Cold War, such as the 1954 government takeover in Guatemala, and the failed intervention in Cuba in 1961. The Shah turned out to be a brutal, arbitrary dictator whose secret police (known as the SAVAK) tortured and murdered thousands of people. Meanwhile, the Iranian government spent billions of dollars on American-made weapons, while the Iranian economy suffered.

In July 1979, the revolutionaries forced the Shah to disband his government and flee to Egypt. The new leader, a radical cleric, Ayatollah Khomeini, installed a militant Islamist government in its place. In October 1979, President Carter agreed to allow the exiled leader to enter the U.S. for treatment of an advanced malignant lymphoma. It was like throwing "a burning branch into a bucket of kerosene." Anti-American sentiment in Iran exploded. Pro-Ayatollah students smashed the gates and scaled the walls of the American embassy in Tehran. Once inside, they seized 66 hostages. Diplomatic maneuvers had no discernible effect on the Ayatollah's anti-American stance; neither did economic sanctions such as the seizure of Iranian assets in the United States. By the Fall of 1980, 44 hostages remained in Iran, but in April, Carter launched Operation Eagle Claw, a risky rescue operation hindered by weather, and after 8 servicemen were killed in the attempt, the operation was aborted.

I knew who Ronald Reagan was, never really liked him as an actor, and knew he had been a Democrat governor in California. Carter's Iranian mess was an opening for Reagan, now a Republican, and he won the election by a landslide. Carter's legacy remained a failed foreign policy, a lost Panama Canal, and the beginning of the Community Reinvestment Act that would eventually cause a major economic collapse.

Though I was aware of the way politics affected our personal lives, I still wasn't involved as an activist, and though angry about so many things the government seemed to be involved in, I wasn't quite angry enough to take any action. I was just 30 years old, my peak years in work and my personal life, and all I heard was how bad Reagan's trickle down economics was, and how terrible it was that he was elected.

I was living in Buffalo, New York, close to my hometown geographically, but far left in cultural and political activities. I was, like most of my peers, busy with life and apathetic to politics.

America seemed to still be a place of relative peace. I could walk to the store at night without fear. My kids could play outside without fear. Race relations had settled down from the '64 Civil Rights movement, and the children of the radical sixties were my age, busy, and perfectly willing to let the government govern. I awoke each morning thinking about my day, the weekend, the holidays and birthdays. I didn't turn on the news or get the paper. I listened to music or to nothing at all.

Then one day, Reagan was shot by John Hinckley, Jr. He survived the attempt on his life, but for a brief moment, George Bush might have become President. The Kennedy assassination popped back into my mind. It was then I remembered all I had read about George H. W. Bush.

Bush had been the director of the CIA, and I was now smart enough to know how involved the CIA was in so many countries, so much of our global presence. Bush had been a part of covert operations, supposedly an economics major, and he was now the Vice President. The whole tangled web in Washington began getting much more clear. Nixon and Bush were connected, Johnson and Nixon were connected, and now Reagan was connected to Bush. Gerald Ford, who served after Carter, was supposed to be the V.P. even though there were difficulties between him and Reagan, but out of nowhere, a surprise to many, Reagan named Bush his V.P. after his primary nomination.

Did Bush want Reagan dead? Bush was fighting over foreign policy even before he was named as Reagan's V.P. He was a globalist, a New World Order progressive, as many Republicans were and are today. Alexander Haig was Reagan's Secretary of State, more conservative in many ways than Bush. The decision to give one or the other control of foreign policy was up in the air at the time of the shooting, but handed to Bush when Reagan returned to the White House.

Bush also had ties to Lee Harvey Oswald, as did Richard Nixon, and was in Dallas the day Kennedy was shot. He was in charge, through the CIA, of Cuban recruitment for the planned attack on Cuba that Kennedy opposed.

It was all such a web and I was increasingly frustrated in trying to find the truth. I studied presidents from decades before, looking for the webs they were in or a part of, searching for answers I instinctively knew I would never find. I knew the JFK assassination changed America, but I was realizing America had been going through a transformation for decades, not evolving, but being transformed covertly. Woodrow Wilson got us into the Federal Reserve and began the progressive tax. He lied to people to get elected and got us into WWI after the Lusitania was sunk by the Germans. There were many communists in America at the time, possibly an outgrowth of the Fabian Socialists, and America was very much an isolationist country preferring to stay out of European affairs. The "Bonus Army" was born out of financial promises, and volunteers loaded ships to help fight with the British. They were promised certificates when they returned to get them back to work and as a payment for their service. Congress, in many votes, refused to fund them and the new President told them to go home. They didn't. Their certificates would mature in 25 years and up to 20,000 had found their way to Washington. The country was still trying to work its way out of Wilson's depression, so Herbert Hoover opposed paying veterans, especially if they weren't wounded. The White House proposed troops to make them leave, but most stayed and continued to rally while living in tent cities surrounding the Capitol.

Surprisingly, it was General MacArthur, not yet an icon of WWII, who finally led armed forces against the veterans, burning their tents, makeshift shelters, and many of the buildings they were occupying. In the end, one veteran was killed and more than 50 were wounded. Most of the veterans returned home by any means they could find, but by the time newly elected Roosevelt took office, more than a thousand had returned to Washington.

FDR needed to quell the violence to impose his agenda, so he started the Citizen's Conservation Corp, made up of about 25,000 veterans to work in the forests. Realizing he too, would veto any bill for aid, the veterans took the offer and disbanded.

CHAPTER 3

My Reagan years were a time of working extra hours in a State University system that was mostly liberal. I had achieved my liberal arts degree, a double major Bachelor of Arts, and had left the Women's Studies program because my allegiance to my country and our constitution was far different from those who worked there. Most of them were students, and of course, most of them were women. We had marched for Title IX, something I did believe in, but their ideology was based on the guidance of far left faculty who followed Marx, Mao, and socialist Viet Nam. Marines had fought the North Vietnamese, and I was a part of a program that supported that enemy. The amazing thing to me regarding their support of this ideology was that Confucius was who they followed, and the women's role in that society was far from liberated or equal. My own brand of what they might label as feminism was to empower women, help them find a voice as women, not as men-wannabes.

I was working non-traditional jobs, non-traditional because they were male dominated. In fact, I was the first woman to repair mainframe computers for IBM, and the first woman at SUNY

Buffalo to hold an engineer position in the computer center. That didn't mean I had broken some glass ceiling as liberals have imagined. It meant I was comfortable in my own skin, and took the training I received in both the Marines and in college seriously.

Was their sexism? Absolutely. In the late seventies, computer rooms in many corporations were off limits to females, and hardware engineers had to be male. If I was scheduled to work overnight to do a machine upgrade, management had a hard time finding another engineer to work with me. Their wives were fearful of overnight work with a woman. I fought off advances, and carried a tool bag with a gun for my late- night service calls. The feminists didn't like that very much. They thought guns were too dangerous. I agree. They are. They're supposed to be. I had to trek through alleys at two in the morning, dressed for success with a tool bag that looked like a briefcase in hand. If someone pulled a gun on me, I would answer with my own. After all, wasn't one of the reasons the second amendment of the constitution was written was so we could protect ourselves? Our homes? Our family? The main reason, of course, was to protect ourselves from our government. The Revolution was fought by common men, and women, against the tyranny of a king and his military subjects, against taxation without representation, and ultimately for freedom.

My time with women's studies ended because I believed in the Constitution, and my right to carry a gun was guaranteed by that document. I was demonized by that large community of women who followed doctrines they didn't even understand. Many of them wanted to go to Viet Nam and live among the people. None of them ever saluted the flag or wept at our anthem. Many were New York Jewish women, some orthodox. Some fought with each other about Palestine and the Jewish state of what is now Israel. A few of the women were black, one a very good friend, but even she decided my allegiance to freedom wasn't something she could support

"But, why, Wanda?" I asked. "Why would you turn on me knowing that black women have tried to free themselves for decades? Following beliefs and tenets that are oppressive to women doesn't make sense to me."

"Because," she answered. "White people owned us, they owned us as slaves. So, these women are mostly white, but they are against racism. They vote the way I vote and feel the way I feel. They know oppression and they fight against it."

"What oppression?" I asked. "They're all middle class or upper middle- class women, half of them from New York, and they're here because they're in college. That's oppression? Their parents expected them to get a college degree, mine didn't. Their parents paid their way. Mine didn't."

She thought for a moment and I felt she was trying to at least keep an open mind.

"Were your parents Democrats?

Are you?"

I shook my head. "No. They're Republican, but what difference does that make?"

"Republicans were the first slave owners. Republicans were the KKK. Republicans made us sit at the back of the bus and kept us out of schools, and wouldn't drink from the same fountain."

I shook my head in disbelief. "Not true, Wanda. Not true. The first slave owner in the United States was black. Slaves were sold by blacks in Africa. The KKK was all democrats because they wanted to keep you down, just use you when they needed you. I don't know the whole history. I don't think anyone ever taught us the whole truth, but I know enough to know you're wrong. Republicans voted to disband the KKK. Republicans voted for the civil rights act in 1964. Democrats voted no."

She looked at me in a way I hadn't seen before. She was listening. She loved me as a friend and she listened. "But what about Martin Luthor King? He was a Democrat and a great man."

"I don't know everything I should about Reverend King, Wanda. I wish I did. I don't think he was a Democrat, but I also don't think he was a Republican. Everyone always tries to box people in. I think he was a Southern Baptist who believed in independence, and if he was alive, I think he'd tell black people to never vote for any party, but to vote for the values being presented, to vote according to the content of the person's character."

"I don't know who's right or wrong," she said. "I know you'd never lie to me or lead me wrong. I wish I knew the truth, the real truth, and could trust it."

I thought about Lyndon Johnson and his progressive push for the black vote. Poverty in the inner cities was rampant, but always worse with blacks. I took my friends hand and looked her in the eye.

"Trust me," I said. "Lyndon Johnson said long ago he'd keep blacks, well he often used the word niggers, voting democrat for 200 years. He may or may not have said those exact words. I do know that before he was President and was in Congress, he voted always with the Southern Democrats against any kind of civil rights for blacks. As President, he needed the votes. They've used you. For votes. Promising you housing and jobs and wealth. He was right. Blacks vote for democrats. And when they're in office, be it mayors or governors or presidents, where do blacks end up?"

She lowered her head as a tear streamed down her cheek. "I guess that's why I'm only one of three in the program. Well, now maybe there'll be only two."

I returned to work the next morning in time to overhear a black joke from a white man to a small group of black men. I watched for reactions and wasn't surprised that the black men laughed. Then, a woman who was also walking by, stopped and interrupted the group. I couldn't hear all she was saying, but I did hear her call the white man racist. The other men shook their heads and seemed to be trying to tell her otherwise, but her arrogance prevailed. She succeeded in shaming the white man. I wondered if she knew the damage she had done to the black men. By assuming racism, she had made them inferior, not only to her, but to all white people. She undermined the non-racial relationship this group had by asserting her presumed authority on what constituted racism.

We had come a long way since Woodrow Wilson. Wilson was a democrat elected in New Jersey, but he was the first southern-born president of the post- civil war period. The South in the early 1900's was mostly Democrat. During the Reconstruction period of 1865–1877, federal law provided civil rights protection in the U.S. South for freedmen, the African Americans who had formerly been slaves, and former tree blacks. In the 1870s, Democrats gradually regained power in the Southern legislatures, having used insurgent paramilitary groups, such as the White League and Red Shirts, to disrupt Republican organizing, run

Republican officeholders out of town, and intimidate blacks to suppress their voting.

Extensive voter fraud was also used. White Democrats had regained political power in every Southern state. These Southern, white, Democratic Redeemer governments legislated Jim Crow laws, officially segregating black people from the white population. Why didn't blacks know that?

Establishment Democrats were passing laws to make voter registration and electoral rules more restrictive, with the result that political participation by most blacks and many poor whites began to decrease. Between 1890 and 1910, ten of the eleven former Confederate states, starting with Mississippi, passed new constitutions or amendments that effectively disenfranchised most blacks and tens of thousands of poor whites through a combination of poll taxes, literacy and comprehension tests, and residency and record-keeping requirements.

Wilson introduced segregation in federal offices, despite much protest from Black American leaders and groups. He appointed Democrat, segregationist Southern politicians because of his own firm belief that racial segregation was in the best interest of black and European Americans alike. He also profiled to maintain segregation within the government. He demanded photographs of those wishing to be employed so he could separate whites from blacks. His tenure as president was part of the Progressive Era, and the beginning of the disenfranchisement of both blacks and poor whites by the Democrat party, not only in the South, but nationwide.

I had survived 4 years of Ronald Reagan and wasn't surprised when he was re-elected. My days now were filled with children, not mine, but throwaways and non-returnables. I volunteered at a runaway home, a place kids ended up for a short period of time before they were either placed in detention, returned home, or returned to the streets. I also worked with battered women shelters, that feminist part of me still hoping to empower more women. On top of that and working, I had kids of my own to raise. Like most parents, I wanted to make sure my kids had a better life than I did, even though I didn't think my life had been so bad.

My politics changed to being more international since one of my kids had Chilean blood. Life in America was always so full that Americans didn't seem to think about life anywhere else, or how we affected a country. My Chilean daughter born in the USA made me learn and come to terms with more that our government was involved with, and none of it made me proud.

I needed to take my daughter back to Chile to find her roots and experience her culture, but the Chile I was about to visit wasn't the Chile I wanted her to know. As I researched where we would stay and people who promised to meet us there, I was struck by the names of many streets and roads. Rockefeller Boulevard? Kissinger Way?

When I traveled to Chile in 1976, I was very naïve about the events taking place there. I was twenty-six with friends from many places. One of those friends was a woman who had been basically deported when her visa expired, even though her ex-husband was still allowed to stay as a college professor and her daughter was born on American soil. She returned to Chile with her daughter and asked me to come to see her country, and to learn. She told me to warn others from home that if I didn't return as scheduled, they should notify the State Department. That in itself was educational because I couldn't imagine an American having trouble traveling anywhere.

I flew from Buffalo, New York, changed planes in New York City, watched a thunderstorm from above over Cuba, and landed in Bogota, Columbia for another plane change. Culture shock was an understatement as I departed the plane on the tarmac far from the tiny terminal and had to walk past burned out planes left over from wars I knew nothing about. The heavily armed Columbian military was the only presence, and the language barrier made any questions difficult. I somehow managed to get directions to a rest room, and then made the long walk again to my Lan Chile Airlines plane.

When I arrived in Santiago, Chile, my friend and her family were outside the glass at the terminal to greet me. The military again was the first sight when I deplaned. I didn't pay much attention because I was excited to be there and her family greeted me as if they had known me forever.

The next few days were spent getting to know the history of Santiago, and it was then I realized I had arrived during the height of the transformational coup that ousted the Socialist leader, Allende. Chile had a new dictator, Augusto Pinochet, and what I learned from those first few days not only frightened me, but regenerated my anger toward my own government, especially the CIA.

My friend, Ana, explained that Allende's form of socialism wasn't like Cuba's or Russia's, and the people were mostly pleased with him as their leader. The problem, she said, was the American government. Allende's democratic election frightened the financial interests in America. Allende's inauguration, in the minds of Nixon and Kissinger, could set a precedent for other governments to follow the same model. That model could allocate resources differently to satisfy agendas, and that would affect over a

billion dollars in American investments.

Henry Kissinger went against the advice of the State Department and enlisted the CIA for a covert operation to end Allende's rule. Nixon made it clear to the entire National Security Council that the policy would be to bring Allende down. "Our main concern," he stated, "is the prospect that he can consolidate himself and the picture projected

to the world will be his success."

Kissinger then sent secret instructions to his ambassador to

convey to Pinochet. "Our strongest desire is to cooperate closely

and establish a firm basis for a cordial and a most constructive

relationship." When his assistant secretary of state for inter-

American affairs asked him what to tell Congress about the reports

of hundreds of people being killed in the days following the coup,

he issued these instructions: "I think we should understand our

policy-that however unpleasant they act, this government is better

for us than Allende was." The United States assisted the Pinochet

regime in consolidating, through economic and military aide,

diplomatic support and CIA assistance in creating Chile's infamous

secret police agency, DINA.

Ana took me to different spots along the Mapocho River

that runs through the heart of Santiago. Blood-stained walls were

evidence of mutilated bodies thrown in the river for all Chileans to

see. She took me past the stadium, though I was cautioned to not

try to take pictures, and told me of the thousands of Chileans and

nationals from other countries who were taken there, tortured, and killed. Those "nationals" included Americans, and Henry Kissinger was directly responsible for their deaths.

I couldn't believe our Republican government was responsible for the coup, but the evidence was right in front of me. I learned later that Kissinger was part of the Bilderberg group, an assembly of elite bankers, power brokers, and elected elites who met once a year to determine the global agenda favorable to their own interests.

When Ana and I took a bus to Valparaiso, both of us noticed two shadowy figures that seemed to be watching us as we dined with a friend of hers.

"Don't let them know you see them," she said. "Act like an American tourist."

I was a tourist, the uneducated, uninformed American who thought America only did good things in the world. We had fought the Germans and won. We had fought the Japanese who attacked us, and won. We helped rebuild Japan after we dropped the bombs to end the war. We did save millions of lives with those bombs and I thought it was our American generosity, coupled with a little guilt, that made us want to help rebuild what we had damaged. We weren't imperialists when we entered WWII, but the FDR regime was a democratic socialist empire that reduced Americans to poverty in a depression, and capitalized on foreign investments that made millions for bankers, Wall Street, and the elites who felt they deserved to be paid, be rich, because they did the work to change our society. Now we had toppled an elected Socialist and replaced him with a military dictator.

We were stopped many times when we traveled by car, at military checkpoints with guns pointed at our windows. They looked for cameras, guns and any other thing they believed to be contraband, and I was no longer sure I was safe, or that Ana and her family were safe. I vowed to get them out of Chile and back to America using any resources I could, but first I had to make that trip myself.

When it was time for my departure, the whole family took me to the airport and then translated so I could get my return ticket validated. In English, they told me that the ticket counter told them I was not on the manifest for the flight. They showed them my unvalidated ticket, but he shook his head and told them I never arrived, according to the manifest. They argued that I must have arrived because I was standing in front of them, but the ticket master said my ticket was a fake, I was not on the manifest, and I should leave the terminal.

"I warned you this might happen," Ana said. "They know your history at Women Studies, your politics, and you are not trusted."

We returned to her parent's home and brainstormed for a way for me to get out. My idea was a cultural one. We called the airport and asked for the full name of the terminal manager. The usual way of asking to speak to anyone was by surname only, Senor whoever.

The following morning, we called and asked for that manager by his full name, a signal that the call was important and that I must be a priority. We told him I was from the American embassy and that his name had been given to me to secure passage out of Chile. In less than a minute, I was given instructions to return to the airport the next day, ask for him, and I would be on my way. When we returned, everything went smoothly, and I was put on a large plane with only seven other passengers en route to Sao Paulo, Brazil.

From Sao Paulo we flew to Miami, still a large plane with a handful of us aboard. As we passed over Cuba, the flight attendant came through the cabin and sprayed everything in sight with something that immediately made me deathly ill. I spent almost the entire trip in the bathroom, and arrived home a very green color that scared those who came to greet me. It took more than three weeks for any of my luggage to arrive, all of it torn to pieces as they looked for whatever they were looking for.

And now, I was about to return to help my child find her roots. Pinochet was still in power, though the atrocities of the postcoup years had lessened. After I had left the first time, Ana's house was invaded by the military, her phone lines cut and dogs dispatched to search in every corner. Her 6 year old daughter was cornered while playing with a friend in the neighborhood and was returned home by a military jeep. She screamed as she entered the house and it took some time to find out what had happened. The Junta guards had them cornered and asked the boy playmate where his father was. When he continuously answered that he didn't know, they shot him and left him there dead in the lot. They loaded Amalia into the jeep and dropped her at home, a signal to her whole family that they would be next if they tried to give me or anyone else information or materials that were against the Pinochet regime.

It became increasingly more obvious to me that our so called foreign relations had nothing to do with political parties, but more with the ideology of globalization and the vying for power within that context. Both Republican and Democrat leaders and presidents were involved in changing regimes of other countries for profit, and the CIA had become a rogue element of our government, led by the policies of puppet masters more than any influence from the American people. Trade agreements seemed to be the course of action for any relationship, some of them helpful to a few, many of them not helpful to any. The party lines so many still believed in were no longer existent after the JFK assassination, and had actually diminished long before that under FDR, Wilson and even Teddy Roosevelt.

I decided it wasn't in the best interest of my daughter, a daughter actually once removed, to return to Chile while so many things were still chaotic. I, instead, embarked on getting her true,

biological mother to America where she would be relatively safe.

CHAPTER 4

I settled back into my work, grateful that I could awaken every day not very worried about anything political. Reagan had a calming effect, on me anyway, and I was a nature lover who just wanted to enjoy God's gifts. I was in an apartment complex across from a beautiful church. I didn't know the denomination because it didn't matter to me. What mattered was the architecture and the surroundings that helped feed my spirit. I was in a lower apartment facing the courtyard, which wasn't ideal, and saw an opening to move upstairs with French doors opening to that church. I leaped at the chance and readied for my move. A friend from D.C. called to see if she could move back to Buffalo and take my apartment. It was no problem. The superintendent knew me well and was thankful he wouldn't have to advertise. I moved in within a week and got busy trying to get Ana back to America.

Because I worked at a university, I had connections that might get her back on a student visa. I asked many people and finally got some answers from the honors department. They knew me well, not just for my computer work with them, but also because I had graduated with a double degree and made Phi Beta

Kappa. We spoke at length about Ana's dilemma, and I found that only if she was applying for a Ph.D. program, could I get her any help. So, now what? I couldn't really communicate with Ana because the mail was censored and phone calls were on delay so authorities in Chile could monitor calls. I trusted she was doing her part on her side of the world, and hoped she trusted me to do mine.

I soon realized I was becoming a "player." I needed to play one department at the university against another, probably lie a little, see if I needed to bribe anyone in Chile, and then wait for the outcome. I almost laughed because I had learned so well from my government research that being a player seemed easy.

I went to Women's Studies and talked to a few who still spoke to me. They said they were trying for a Ph.D. program in their senior department, but weren't sure when it was coming through or if it would at all. Women's Studies was now under American Studies to make degrees easier to get. How sad that was to me. A department that had been born of excellence and should have been empowering women was becoming nothing more than an indoctrination course for the left.

47

"Keep your eye out for the FBI," one woman told me. "They've had infiltrators and we lost one of our women to suicide because of them."

"Suicide? Oh, my God! Who?

How?"

"Tara," she answered. "Remember her? Short, a little round? Somehow they got to her and had her reporting to them about what articles we shared and what we were teaching. I guess it got the best of her because she was turning in friends, so she ended it."

"That doesn't sound right," I said. "She was tough. How did she do it?"

"Pills. That's what I heard anyway. She wandered around during a snowstorm and died under a snow mound. They didn't find her until it thawed a little."

I thought of all the mysterious, but uninvestigated, deaths I had read about in my research, and felt amazed that those same scenarios of big government could possibly be the same for us little people. I didn't believe the suicide. Someone either drugged her with an overdose, or filled her with pills and led her to that place near the lake.

I returned to the honors department and told them I needed the paperwork for Ana to get her visa for the Ph.D. program in Women's Studies. I had filled out her application and I handed it to my friend behind the counter.

"Oh. No signature from the department. We have to have that," she said.

I acted very flustered, even cursed myself out loud for the effect. "My fault," I said. "I was supposed to wait for the signature and got a call about a down computer. Damn! I don't know when I can get back over there."

My friend thought for a moment, checked some boxes, and smiled. "Not a problem," she said. "We'll sign it here so we can get it in the works."

I thanked her profusely, said a little prayer for forgiveness for my lie, and went on my way to write to Ana.

"It won't be long now," I wrote. I needed to be cryptic in case my letter was opened either here or there. "They need you desperately here and they're handling the paperwork. You should have a call from the embassy soon."

I finally had time to relax in my new apartment. I opened the French doors to a cool breeze, piled pillows on the floor, and just listened to the whispers of the trees. I felt like I shouldn't care about what was happening in Washington, or Paris, ,or somewhere in Russia. A part of me wanted to detach from everything and everyone and just enjoy my life. I had a job, a nice place to live, money in the bank. I didn't need politics. Then I remembered a book I had read for Women's Studies, Mao's Little Red Book, the Communist handbook for China. One thing he said hit home. "The personal is political." Of course, that meant the political was also personal. If Senators decided we should be taxed for something, then that became personal. If my friend thought she needed an abortion, then that became political. There was no real way to avoid politics, only the level of engagement. Americans can be selfish when it comes to that. I don't think they always were. I remember times when it seemed everyone cared about everyone in one way or another. Sure, we had after school fights and we all called each other names, but when the chips were down, we stood together.

Bullying wasn't called that in my school. If bullying meant the weak guy picking on the different guy to prove he wasn't the weak guy, then we all knew who they were and why they did it. One bully surrounded by ten or twenty kids who wouldn't stand for it suddenly became a nice guy or an invisible one. We didn't need the government to tell us how to get along or settle differences. The teachers were our only governors, and they were very good at their jobs. The whole thing was so easy, if you just followed the rules. We knew if we didn't, there were consequences and none of us wanted to lose our freedom. We were engaged, in relationships with each other, friendships that would last for decades, built on trust and truth and honor.

I watched the trees sway past the church steeple and thought about my daughter and the other kids. I wasn't sure they understood honor. I knew they would never lie to me. That was learned very early. But I wasn't sure they had the role models or teaching to know honor. I had used the honors department to secure safe passage for Ana. Was it an honorable thing to do? I could do it because I was held in good standing with the department and the university as a whole. They honored that standing by trusting me. But I had to lie. Where was the honor in lying? There was none. I had to accept that I did what I had to do. I had always told my kids to ask themselves two questions before they said or did anything. Were they coming from love or fear? And was what they were doing or saying in the highest and best interest of everyone, including them?

I loved Ana and I loved her child, but I was also fearful because of the situation in Chile. So, was I lying because I feared for her, or because I loved her? There was no fear for me. I was safe. So, I must be coming from love for her. Was lying in the best interest of everyone, including me? If I hadn't lied, Ana might not have any other way to escape Chile and be with her family here, so it was in their best interest. It was in my best interest because I was helpless against the junta and had exhausted any other way. Was it honorable? Not to me. It was the first time in my life I had lied about anything, and I promised myself it would be the last.

My friend from D.C. moved into my old apartment and totally settled in. She wanted to be a lawyer, had the money to do it, and was back home nearer to friends and family. It was nice to have her in the same building and I looked forward to just hanging out.

Life doesn't always work according to plan. I fell asleep gazing out my French doors, but suddenly awoke with a feeling something was wrong. I was sweaty, scared, confused. I took some deep breaths to calm myself down, but couldn't get rid of the feeling of danger somewhere.

As a child, I was raised by Seneca Nation grandmothers. My family abandoned me at ten and I slept in a cemetery for many years, the safest place to be. I cut my hand badly one day, washed it with water and bandaged it with a rag I found. A few days later, my infection was obvious. I didn't have family or a doctor and my friends knew that. One of them told me to go to the reservation and see the grandmothers. It was a short trip, so I washed my swollen, green hand, bandaged it again, and made my way there. There were two elders there to greet me and one took me by my good hand and sat me down where the light was brightest. She removed the bandage without a word, then smiled and nodded at the other woman.

"Close your eyes," she said. "Close your eyes so you don't see the pain. See instead your healthy, strong hand."

I silently obeyed, although I was

a little nervous.

"Now close your ears," she continued, "so you don't remember hearing that you are hurt."

I again obeyed, though it was hard to find a way to not hear anything. I concentrated, pretended I was deaf, and eventually felt the silence. I felt them doing things to my hand, but I stayed as they had ordered. The first woman tapped my shoulder and I woke up as if I'd been sleeping. The wound on my hand was clean. They rubbed something green into it, placed two leaves on it, and wrapped it in clean cloth.

"In two days, your hand will be happy again," said the second elder.

I smiled at both of them incredulously and stood up to leave.

"Wait, Little One," said the first woman. "Let me look again at your other hand."

I opened my hand as she took it in hers and tried to see what she was seeing.

"You have the M," she said. "Do you see it? This line connects to this one and that line to this one. It forms a connected letter M. You have a gift."

I looked at the M, then at her, and then put my hand in my pocket. I didn't know then about gifts and didn't want to know.

"Little One, you are special. You have the gift. You have many gifts. We can teach you, help you to see them and use them."

I didn't know what they were saying, but they convinced me to return as soon as I could. And so I did. They taught me about herbs and medicinal plants, how to get the oil from them, the "lifeblood." They spent hours telling me about native spirits, the four directions, our connection to all things and that all things have spirit. We spoke of animals and all we could learn from them, and then we spoke about the gift of intuition. It wasn't intuition the way most people think. I was very intuitive and had already learned how to tap into that. They wanted me to know about my medical intuition, a way of knowing what was out of balance in someone. They cautioned me not to take on the illnesses or imbalances of others, but to recognize their energy within me and then let it go.

"When you feel your attachment to someone, look for the clues being given to you. Listen with your heart as you did when you were wounded. Your intuition has many sides and you will know things before they happen, sometimes feel them while they are happening."

I spent many months with my grandmothers, ending up with seven altogether. Each had special strengths and talents. All had special gifts.

I got up and went to the open French doors, listening for the wind or any voice that would tell me what was wrong. I was cold, as if naked on a winter's day. My eyes felt like flames, and my legs hurt as if I had been running.

Suddenly, the phone rang. My friend downstairs had been raped. She eventually got away through an open window, scraping her naked body and falling hard to the ground. She ran until she saw a house with a light on and banged on the door in utter fear.

"We found a sweatshirt and some jeans for her," the man said. "You'd better come and get her."

I took her to the hospital and fought with the doctors to get a female in the room with her. She didn't need strange men checking her, touching her, even if they were doctors. A female nurse and policewoman finally went in the room with her, and I got another friend of ours to come and wait for her while I went looking for the rapist. I was beyond angry, and all my Marine Corps training was right at the surface.

I met the police at the apartment, saw the disarray in the bedroom, checked the window, and followed any clues I could find to track him. I did find which end of the courtyard he went through, and that he might have hopped a bus, but that's as far as I got. It was 4 in the morning and I was supposed to be at work by six, but there was no way I was going to leave until I knew Kathy was okay and back home safe and sound. I didn't want her to return to her apartment because the sight would bring back all the emotional distress and trauma, so she came to my apartment until her family from New York could get there.

Rape was an act of violence toward women, and my rage was almost uncontrollable. It wasn't sex, it was misogyny in its highest and most evil form.

When I was sure Kathy was okay, I drove to work, dazed with anger, unaware of the time or day. I had fought rapists in the Women Marine barracks almost nightly and all that memory, all that rage, was back within me. I got to the computer lab at the university almost two hours late, and was greeted by my manager, an ex- Navy guy who had no degree, less experience, but made a lot more than I did.

"Sorry I'm late," I said matter- of- factly. "My friend was raped and I had to take care of her."

He almost chuckled as he turned to look at me. "Raped? Ha! You know, of course, that most women who get raped ask for it, right?"

I glared at him and clenched myfist around a screwdriver.

"No, they don't, Hank. They don't ask to be violated, beaten, used. They don't rape people, men do. Men who think it gives them power over a female, power over their mothers, a power they will never have because they're men and not women. Women don't ask for rape."

He chuckled again. "Probably dressed sexy, or didn't close the blinds or something."

I flipped the screwdriver in my hand and hurled it at him. It just missed his head and stuck in the wall behind his ear.

"I quit. You've been nothing but a sexist bastard from day one. I could have nailed you. You know what?" I picked up my personal things and headed for the door. "I should have aimed a little to the left, and when they found you, I could have said you asked for it."

I was out of a job. I went back to my apartment and talked to the superintendent about how this guy had gotten into Kathy's apartment, the apartment I had lived in for seven years. The window had no stop locks. There was no alarm system in the building. The lights in the courtyard were dim or missing bulbs. The courtyard itself was easily accessible with no gates or fence. I told the Super I wanted the names and numbers of the owners. They had to address these problems so this didn't happen to someone else.

My letter to them got a quick response that said the building was livable and although some repairs had to be made, my list was far too extensive and didn't warrant extra time.

I immediately called for a meeting of all the apartments in the complex, and most people came to the basement to find out what I had to say.

"The landlords are telling me they don't have to make needed repairs, things that need to be done for our safety, security, health and wellbeing. I've spoken to a lawyer and there are things we can do to change this, but we need to stick together."

People asked why all of a sudden this was an issue, why was I taking it on, how were they involved and what good would it do. I realized at that moment I was again on a mission and I intended to win.

"A woman was raped here last week," I said. "A man came through her window and attacked her for almost two hours. No one heard her screams. No one saw him. When I spoke to people to see what they saw or knew, I got an earful on needed repairs, lights that don't work, leaky ceilings, doorbells that don't work, no security lights, no alarms, and on and on. When I forwarded that list to the landlords, they responded with typical arrogance and refused to take action. So, we'll take action instead.

We can pay our rent into an escrow account, dated with everyone's name and amount paid. They don't get rent until they do their job. We'll form a tenant's association, something Americans should have done a long time ago. These guys want to be slumlords, just like the government does in our cities. We're supposed to pay rent, or in the government's case, taxes, and all they have to do is receive our money and spend it on whatever they want. They don't spend our rent on our homes, our premises. We can do this until they start doing what needs to be done."

It took a few weeks, but most tenants came onboard. We picketed, believing that demonstrations made a difference. We were interviewed by newspapers and television, believing that media exposure would pressure the landlords. We were told to just move somewhere else by those who weren't experiencing our complaints

. Finally, the 4 landlords asked for a meeting with our lawyers and theirs. I met with them at a safe office space, and met the three other landlords for the first time. We had demanded a building inspector. His findings listed more than a hundred violations. We had put our rents in escrow for more than 5 months, so the landlords were feeling the money pinch. When I sat down at the table, one of them crossed his legs to reveal a gun holstered at his ankle. It was a deliberate exposure proven by his statement to me.

"You seem to like shooting your mouth off," he said. "We're losing our patience with this crap."

I told them all we would continue withholding rent until they came up to code according to the violation report. The only other alternative was a day in court.

We were scheduled for a court date within a week and many of the tenants came to support me as the spokesman. When the judge entered, he immediately told me to report to his chambers "without counsel." My lawyers didn't object very loudly so I had no choice. When I entered his chambers, three of the landlords' attorneys were there, and so were the landlords. The judge didn't ask any questions. He, instead, gave his ruling.

"You will release all money from the escrow account of the Main-Jewett Tenant's Association and pay that money to the rightful parties. You will cease and desist any demonstrations on or near the premises. You will disband the tenant's association and hold no further meetings. You will cease and desist from any media interviews, be they written newspaper, radio, television, flyers or any other means. You will have 30 days to vacate the premises or be physically ejected and held in contempt of court."

After a moment of silent glares, I said, "I'd like my attorneys here. This makes no sense."

"Here is the sense," he said in a commanding voice. "I have ruled. If you fail to comply, I will prosecute every tenant who is currently on rent control for failure to pay and have them removed from the premises."

"You can't do that! That's against the law!" I want to appeal your decision."

"You're very brave," he said, leaning across the desk. "You see, I AM the law here, and if you don't think I'll prosecute, just try me."

I thought about his demands and asked myself the two questions. Was I coming from love or fear? I wasn't afraid of him, but I was fearful he'd follow through. Most of the rent control tenants were elderly, many of them women. They supported the efforts of the association because they had lived there for years without proper maintenance. I was fearful for them because I loved them.

Would my compliance be in the best and highest interest of all, including me? I decided it was in the best interest of most of the tenants, if not all, and though I'd have to move, I didn't know where that move would take me.

"Do you understand me?" He demanded.

I nodded my head in the affirmative.

"Okay. You will not speak of anything that occurred in these chambers and will comply when I call you to the bench."

With that, I was led back to the courtroom to await his public decision. When the court was called to order, his decision was verbatim, except for the not speaking to anyone part. I was forced to say, "Yes, Sir," in front of tenants and friends with no explanation as to why I would comply. I was then led through a side door to a separate hallway where I slumped to the floor in exhaustive tears.

One of my non-tenant friends found me and asked what happened. I told her I didn't know if I could tell her because I didn't want any negative consequences. She then told me the judge was up for re-election and she had seen him joking and shaking hands with the landlords.

"So, they bought him," I said.

I had done the honorable thing, protected the elderly tenants even though they thought I let them down. Eventually, many of the repairs were done. The building inspector retired one day before the court date and in the days preceding court, I had almost been run over downtown, my car was destroyed by repeated collision with one vehicle, my mail was lost or opened and my phone had many hang ups. So, in the end, I had done what was best for everyone, including me, and that tenant's association became the model for neighborhood watches and other associations that stopped a high percentage of crime and enlivened many neighborhoods.

As I thought about it, the whole process was very much a microcosm of the macrocosm. The same corruption, deceit and lawlessness I had researched and lived through on a larger scale, was very personal in my life, and the personal had, indeed, become political.

CHAPTER 5

I moved into a new apartment via the benefit of retirement savings and began looking for work. Ana was due to arrive from Chile in a month as long as there were no glitches with the embassies, and Reagan was in his second term, embroiled in a new scandal.

Ronald Reagan's efforts to eradicate Communism spanned the globe, but the insurgent Contras' cause in Nicaragua was particularly dear to him. Battling the Cuban-backed Sandinistas, the Contras were, according to Reagan, "the moral equivalent of our Founding Fathers." Under the so-called Reagan Doctrine, the CIA trained and assisted this and other anti-Communist insurgencies worldwide. What assisting meant was providing financial assistance, but this was almost impossible because the Democrats were now in control of congress after the 1982 elections. In 1985, while Iran and Iraq were at war, Iran made a secret request to buy weapons from the United States. McFarlane, Reagan's National Security Advisor, sought Reagan's approval, in spite of the embargo against selling arms to Iran. McFarlane explained that the sale of arms would not only improve U.S. relations with Iran, but might in turn lead to improved relations with Lebanon, increasing U.S. influence in the troubled Middle East. Reagan's main focus was securing the release of seven American hostages held in Lebanon. He felt he had a duty as President to bring those hostages home, and because of that, violated his own oath of truth, and the support of the American public.

The arms-for-hostages proposal divided the administration. Longtime policy adversaries Secretary of Defense Caspar Weinberger and Secretary of State George Shultz opposed the deal, but Reagan, McFarlane and CIA director William Casey supported it. With the backing of the president, the plan progressed. By the time the sales were discovered, more than 1,500 missiles had been shipped to Iran. Three hostages had been released, only to be replaced with three more, in what Secretary of State George Shultz called "a hostage bazaar."

When the Lebanese newspaper "Al-Shiraa" printed an exposé on the clandestine activities in November, 1986, Reagan went on television and vehemently denied that any such operation had occurred. He retracted the statement a week later, insisting that the sale of weapons had not been an arms-for-hostages deal. Despite the fact that Reagan defended the actions by virtue of their good intentions, his honesty was doubted. Polls showed that only 14 percent of Americans believed the president when he said he had not traded arms for hostages. As a somewhat strong Reagan supporter, I was not only disappointed, but angry. I agreed the return of hostages was important, but I disagreed with any kind of deals to do so.

Then there was the problem of missing funds. Only two million of the reported thirty million the Iranians had paid for missiles was accounted for. Lieutenant Colonel Oliver North, believing he had Reagan's blessing, diverted much of the money to the anti-communists, the "Contras" in Nicaragua who were fighting the Cuban-backed rebels. Because Congress had specifically stopped many CIA –backed operations, North felt he had to use what resources he could find to aid the Contras.

Of course, Reagan's Vice President was George H.W. Bush, the ex-CIA director who had been involved in anti-Cuban covert operations for now two decades. North was fired, as were many others involved, but no evidence pointed to Reagan knowing about the diversion of money.

I watched Reagan's denials on television and continued to follow his radio addresses, a constant way to stay informed when you're busy working or traveling. Then one day he announced his war on drugs, or more notably, his wife Nancy's war on drugs. Cocaine use and trafficking was at an all time high and the new slogan for children to learn was, "Just say no."

I had never been a drug user, nor a drinker. Because of my past with Native America learning earth medicine at a young age, I wasn't interested in anything that could alter my mind or destroy my body. I listened to God and felt Him guide me. I often would walk up to strangers who were hurting from a sore shoulder or battered knee, anything that I felt within me was bothering them, and then did what I could through body alignment, massage or just touch to alleviate their pain. I never asked for payment because I had been told to only receive, never ask, so more often than not, I would just walk away without another word.

When it came to drug companies, that was a different story. I had developed an introductory holistic health course and presented it to many in the Western New York area and several other states. I knew pharmaceutical companies stemmed from the Rockefellers, and the many from Germany who were brought here to continue their experimentation in labs. Pharmaceutical companies and the health care system were worse than any oil company or bank for fleecing Americans. They dealt in fear and dependency, and the more involved the government got, the higher the costs to consumers. Drug companies exist to keep people sick.

As Reagan's second term began to wind down, there was some change in drug use, but the drug traffic across our borders was increasing, and at the same time, Americans had a new disease to worry about

Reagan didn't really talk much about AIDS, but it had invaded parts of our population and was proving to be deadly.

When pharmaceutical companies finally stepped up to provide some kind of relief or possible cures, the costs of drugs were so outrageous that many who were HIV positive sold their homes, mortgaged their lives, to be able to afford the drugs.

Rockefeller had used his oil money to buy out part of the massive German pharmaceutical cartel, I.G. Farben. This was the very same cartel that would later assist Hitler to implement his eugenics-based vision of a New World Order, so often touted by G.H.W. Bush. It was founded on racial supremacy, by manufacturing chemicals and poisons for war. With the control of drug manufacturing under his wings, Rockefeller then embarked on another plan of action.

Rockefeller saw that there were many types of doctors and healing modalities in existence at that time, from chiropractic to naturopathy to homeopathy to holistic medicine to herbal medicine and more. He wanted to eliminate the competitors of western medicine, the only modality which would propose drugs and radiation as treatment, thus enriching Rockefeller who owned the means to produce these treatments, so he hired a man called Abraham Flexner to submit a report to Congress in 1910.

This report "concluded" that there were too many doctors and medical schools in America, and that all the natural healing modalities which had existed for hundreds or thousands of years, were unscientific quackery. It called for the standardization of medical education, whereby only the allopathic-based AMA be allowed to grant medical school licenses in the US.

Sadly, Congress acted upon the conclusions and made them law. Incredibly, allopathy became the standard mainstream modality, even though its 3 main methods of treatment in the 1800s had been blood-letting, surgery, and the injection of toxic heavy metals like lead and mercury to supposedly displace disease!

Understanding holistic health means understanding your roots and your connection to Earth and heaven. The Earth, we've been taught, is one of nine or more planets in a solar system. It has a history, a geology, a topography and many electro-magnetic forces that create and allow life. It has layers of composition consisting mainly of water and minerals and its core is a mystery to all but the most creative science fiction writers. We know it is somehow connected to God, or whomever we believe created it, and it changes every day. It has within its power the ability to cleanse its rivers and streams, move its magnetic plates and nourish those who live within and on it.

The Earth also has the power to self-destruct and to struggle for survival. It reacts to change, poisons, and man-made obstacles. It dies without water and gasps when it cannot breathe. It has rainbows and stars and warming sun that smiles at us in the morning. It sings, helps birds to soar, cushions our fall, provides our food and heals our wounds. Look in the mirror. Aren't we all a part of this wonder? Don't we also have a history, a genealogy that gives us our birthmark and clues to our beginning? Aren't we all topographic, in different shapes, sizes and colors?

The Earth is 75-80% water. So are we. The Earth's minerals are the same elements that compose the tissues, blood and bones of our bodies. Each of those elements has either a positive or a negative charge and reacts to the magnetic poles and electromagnetic forces within and around us. Our physical selves are very much like the Earth we walk on.

We separate ourselves from the Earth with our minds, of which we consciously use only 8 to 12 %. The mind allows us to create, and provides the stimulus to a network of wires we call nerves to give us movement and the ability to change shape. We can change our minds as quickly as the magnetic forces within us can change direction. We can alter our minds with drugs and close

our minds with prejudice, judgment and bigotry. We can open our

minds to new ideas, new places, new experiences, and seal our

minds when our egos are challenged or afraid. The mind and the

body are a team, and what we think or believe is reflected in our

body language, our walk, our stance and our vision. We see and

hear what we want to and physically react to loud noises, violent

attacks or sad stories. As children, we cried or peed in our pants

when we saw or heard something frightening. Out of trust, we

allowed our minds to be controlled by radio and television,

advertising, and the misguided wisdom of others. Because we gave

up the power to reason for ourselves and have stayed too afraid of

the world, or Hell, or the wrath of God, we have also lost the

power to unconditionally love ourselves and others. We're no

longer in charge of our health or happiness. How often do we

chide the person who has "a mind of his own?" Are we so afraid?

Have we been taught so well to fear instead of love that we no

longer resemble the precious and unique individuals we were

intended to be?

There are only two emotions that truly exist in our lives, fear and love. Emotions are energy in motion. All feelings, thoughts and actions can be reduced to one question. Are we coming from fear or from love? If we are coming from fear, we have a responsibility to face it, overcome it, or change ourselves so we come only from love.

Does the Earth have a soul or a spirit, as we believe we do? Is there anyone who doesn't believe there is a part of us that's untouchable, unknown, unrealized? We have free will, a gift, and the power to choose, but what part of us knows the outcome and the reason? Our spirit is a complicated energy, an appendage of a God that knows all. A whisper, a breeze, a fall day, an eagle's cry, a baby's smile – with each we feel something in our soul. We search for soul mates through dating services or parties and long for the forever relationship that we believe completes us. We attach the heart to the soul in songs and greeting cards, knowing somehow that love is connected to soul and that soul is a good thing. For some there are spirit guides, to others angels, and still others unseen teachers who have the key to our soul and our purpose and help us on our paths. Indeed, the Earth has a soul. It, too, is a unique creation, entrusted with our well-being, unconditionally providing food, water and life, and somewhere deep inside knowing its purpose.

Holistic health, or the wholistic approach to health, considers all of these things when dealing with imbalance. There is no drug or cure for a broken heart, but there are questions to be asked, patterns to be discovered, physical reactions, mindful changes, and spiritual comforts. To approach the body holistically is to encompass and respect the whole being. Our creation began long before our conception and birth. Healthy, balanced parents, both mother and father, are essential to a baby's well-being. If one parent abuses alcohol or drugs, our children will be affected and thus the grandchildren. If one parent takes over-the-counter medications on a regular basis, our livers and interstitial tissues hold the memory. If we are conceived in anger, with guilt, without love, we will live those lessons, and possibly inflict others with the projection of those negative feelings and thoughts. No one of us is alone. No one's life is untouched by others. Each of us is part of a continuous circle, each life cycle learning and building on the one before.

The body has a reason for being, part of which is providing a harbor for the soul. None of us as humans can fulfill our purpose without the body. The energy flowing through us changes and alerts us to imbalances, but we most often choose not to listen. We mask pain with drugs, cover wounds with ointments, repair teeth without questions, and remove organs without respect. What doctor whose Volvo had a check engine light on would remove the engine instead of finding the cause? Most of us take care of and understand our cars and computers better than we do our vital bodies. If you have rotated the tires on your SUV and not looked into how your shoes are affecting your balance or the wear and tear on your back, or if you've changed the oil every three thousand miles because you know it preserves the engine, but haven't paid attention to the oil balance, filters and lubrication of your body, you are one of the millions who believe your body's health and well-being is someone else's job. Are you mystified by computers because you believe they are some grand invention beyond your scope of understanding, or they're electronic monsters you have no use for so don't have to learn? Computers have viruses, worms, bad input, and they "crash." Diagnostics are done and "fixes" are implemented. You were the first computer, with input and output, read-only and random access memory, digital by nature, electronic by design. Demystify your body and take back the power inherently yours. Anatomy is not hard. Physiology is illogical to many, but sensible if you understand circles instead of lines. Pathology is understood by every mother who ever had a sick child.

When you begin to understand your physical being, you can also start to grasp the mental and spiritual sides of you. Together they form a triangle, the most powerful structure on Earth.

The Pyramids remind us of this multidimensional truth. The mind, body, spirit connection is a balanced force and essential to all life. No one side of this triangle should be stronger than the other. When one takes precedence, the other sides have no choice but to collapse. If the spirit is all you concentrate on and you believe that will take care of everything in your life, your body will deteriorate and your mind will confuse you with its own short circuits. If you believe the mind is the only truly powerful part of you, your spirit may falter, and again your body may fail. If you concentrate only on your physical being, your mind and spirit can get confused.

Even two out of three sides doesn't work. It takes three evenly balanced sides to make the triangle.

Most people interchange the words mind and brain, and then many just clump them together into "head." We have headaches, migraine headaches, sinus headaches, tension headaches, allergy headaches, and hangover headaches. The head becomes the scapegoat when, in fact, it's the mind and memory telling the brain to react so that we can determine the cause and alleviate it. The brain is the physical electronic connector box, with millions, perhaps trillions of interactive energy pulses and triggers guiding the body to reaction and function. The brain stem connects to our spinal column, which allows the impulses to travel to every organ, system and structure in the body. When the brain is declared dead, the energy that fuels life is shut off, and the soul/spirit within us leaves the harbor on another journey. Interesting that back surgery often fuses parts of the spine that normally would conduct this energy. Why do we believe this is a viable solution to back pain? Why don't we understand that not only can back pain be coming from spinal misalignment, mineral deficiency, polluted drinking and/or bathing water or a host of other causes, but also may be the body's way of telling us that one of our systems or organs normally innervated or "turned on" by that part of our spine is in trouble or needs attention? The system is out of balance, the mind troubled, the brain reactive and the gift of pain authorized.

When we approach our spiritual side, we often misinterpret this as religion or religious belief. We put our faith in God, pray and hope for relief or salvation. We're grateful when the pain is gone, or thankful for our child's return to health. Our mistake is the commingling of spirit with the institution of religion. In churches, we are once again told what to believe, how to believe, how to behave, how to judge. We're given textbooks, pamphlets, and catechisms with all the rules and laws of living translated and interpreted for us. If we believe in the Commandments, then we should know, as children do, that there are only a few rules to follow, otherwise we're free to do everything else.

Even if we sometimes break those rules, if our intention was love and not fear, we will most likely be forgiven.

We need to understand that modern medicine came under the control of the church in the Middle Ages and remains under the university and church related laws of superiority and treatment. Doctors need not be creative in their treatment of patients or disease if they believe their cohorts and counterparts are the only viable source of information, and that the patient is not trained in medicine, therefore should be ignored. The church separated itself from the actual practice of physical medicine with the Renaissance, but maintains its position as the only authority on spiritual health regardless of denomination. This raises an imbalance with each individual's mind and body, as we are as unique as we are alike. The spiritual side of nature either stands in the forefront or takes a back seat, thus depleting the power of the pyramid or triangle, and rendering us incapable of healing ourselves.

Rockefeller and his buddy, Carnegie, systematically dismantled the curricula of medical schools by removing any mention of the natural healing power of herbs and plants, or of the importance of diet to health. The result is a system which, to this day, churns out doctors who are, almost always, utterly clueless about nutrition, spinal nerve connections to balance, and the healing power of natural plants and oils.

The Hill-Burton Act of 1946 gave hospitals grants for construction and modernization, on the condition they provide free healthcare to anyone in need, without discrimination of any kind. Although there were good sides to this, the downside was that once people had become dependent on this system for their healthcare needs, especially those on pharmaceutical pills which need to be taken day after day without end, the system switched into a paid system, and the Rockefellers found themselves with new lifelong customers.

The bitter truth is that, in general, when you go to your Western doctor, you are seen as a potential market for the medical factory's products. For Big Pharma, there is no financial incentive to heal you, because a patient cured is a customer lost. Even if you are not sick, Big Pharma is still targeting you, trying to convince you that you are ill.

Remember, all these synthetic drugs are isolates. Many are derived from plant compounds, but because Nature cannot be patented and sold, Big Pharma has no interest in natural cures. What they do instead is engage in bio-piracy. They research natural compounds, copy them, modify them in a lab, then try to steal and patent them. If they get a patent, they then market their pill as a wonder drug while simultaneously (through fake scientific research) suppress and criticize the original plant as being worthless, so you won't go to the source of the cure.

I spoke to several men I knew about the spread of the AIDS virus, and in the course of learning it was already devastating our community, I learned even more about the healthcare system. I didn't know why Reagan wasn't concentrating on it, but I assumed it was his politics on homosexuality. Since AIDS was being propagandized as a gay disease, I believe Reagan didn't want any part of it. One of the failures of the Republican party was that they often were too pragmatic and dogmatic in their platforms. They became much too exclusionary when it came to some domestic issues so they could satisfy the religious right.

Another belief I had was that Reagan knew the drug companies would exploit the gay community and the anti-gay electorate. He believed in telling the truth, and by failing to mention what would be soon classified as an epidemic, he maintained the distance necessary to remain truthful.

Nancy's drug war and Ronald's economic policies that brought down the price of gas and reduced taxes, made his popularity jump to new highs as he left office. Reagan had one more giant moment when he demanded of Soviet Premier Gorbachev "Mr. Gorbachev, tear down that wall." The Berlin wall was going to come down and George H. W. Bush got to ride on his coattails.

CHAPTER 6

I was no fan of Bush '41, but voted for him to keep the Democrat, Dukakis, out of office. Voting against the other guy had become the way Americans tried to maintain a voice in our government. The only thing Bush had said during his campaign that I wholeheartedly agreed with was his pledge of no new taxes. When he said, "Read my lips. No new taxes," I didn't really believe him, but, like most Americans, I was still trying to recover from past democrat economies and still waiting for all the Reagan economic policies to prove themselves.

Reagan had rebuilt the military and came from a "peace through strength" vision, but ended his presidency with a large federal deficit that could affect all of us as time went by. Bush's promised tax policy was conservative, but I knew it was impossible to keep that promise. Revenue had to come from somewhere and taxes were always the way.

I actually liked Bush's "Thousand Points of Light" speech at the convention because I had spent most of my life doing exactly what that speech said. But when he included his vision of a new world order, and then later began to put together a North American Treaty with Canada and Mexico, I realized I was witnessing an America no longer there for the people or by the people, but an America led by foreign interests and the rising power of the United Nations. I knew that meant a return to imperialism or totalitarianism, something that Reagan had kept from happening during the cold war with Russia.

Maybe because of the restart of economic growth or because I was just tired of taking calls for computer repairs in the middle of the night, I changed careers just before my father's sudden death. The space program was gaining steam, the collapse of the Soviet Union meant the threat from Russia that had been prevalent since JFK's Bay of Pigs was now gone, and I was ready to learn about money.

I had earned an above- board salary working with computers. In 1971, with salary, overtime, per diem and car allowances, I was making almost $90,000 per year. My healthcare was paid for by my employers, and two weeks paid vacation and holidays made work manageable. By 1988, my income was well into six figures, but, I had nothing to show for it.

Getting Ana out of Chile had cost me thousands of dollars in what could be considered bribes. Raising and caring for a total of 11 children during more than one recession had cost me tens of thousands, if not more.

I realized I was like many women who were never part of the good old boys network in the financial boardrooms or on the floor of the stock exchange, and I didn't like it. I had spent years empowering women to find their voices, but never empowered them to control their checkbooks.

My father died two days after I announced to him that I was going into the financial services industry. I researched the best companies in the field, left my computer career just as the microchip was being born, and joined IDS Financial Services.

I asked them how long it would take to get to management and they said one to two years. That was not acceptable to me. People needed help now, and women, subject to an increased divorce rate, single parenthood, and widowhood, needed help sooner than that.

I got firsthand knowledge of that belief immediately after my father's death. He had cashed in his insurance policies to deal with inflation, lost his business because of taxes during Carter's fiasco presidency, and left my mother with a small insurance policy to bury him. He also left bills behind and as the days after his funeral allowed my mother to try to take control of her life, I found that she didn't even know how to write a check. My father, as did so many other men after WWII, kept control of the finances and checkbook, sometimes revealing nothing about the state of the family affairs.

I learned all I could as quickly as I could and secured all the licenses necessary to become a financial planner. Maybe because I had been on both sides of the computer industry, hardware and software, or because I always found it easy to envision things and create, financial planning was easy.

I grew my client base at record speed and was made a training manager with IDS within six months. My clientele included many from the university system, many women, and a high percentage of liberals or Democrats along with gay men being exploited by lawyers, Jewish men and women who stayed with the stereotype of keeping everything "just in case," and a few right wingers who thought they owned the world.

I learned and developed sales tactics that car salesmen should have known, found out about the real way to buy gold, and realized after a short time that I was changing people's lives.

The liberal women had no clue how to deal with money. Their emphasis in life was social programs, social justice, equality and abortions. It never occurred to them that social programs cost money, until they realized their own finances were in trouble and they had no idea how to fix them. They thought social security would be their retirement plans and maybe pensions from husbands or the university would take up the slack. These were the women who were considered privileged because of their tenured positions, educated and secure in their standings within their communities.

When I made them list their donations, their cash on hand, income, savings plans, retirement plans and investments, it opened their eyes to how they had used emotions and rhetoric, usually from their chosen Democrat candidates, to steer their money away from themselves and into the high tax coffers of the D.C. cartels.

We didn't talk politics, but when their plans got presented to them and they could see the logic and their mistakes from the past, they not only followed through with allocations and direction, but they also maintained a good relationship with me as their planner and, in some instances, mentor.

Then Bush went back on his campaign promise. He faced the problem of what to do with leftover deficits spawned by the Reagan years. At $220 billion in 1990, the deficit had grown to three times its size since 1980 and he was dedicated to curbing the deficit, believing that America could not continue to be a leader in the world without doing so. He began an effort to persuade the Democratic controlled Congress to act on the budget, with Republicans believing that the best way was to cut government spending, and Democrats convinced that the only way would be to raise taxes. Bush accepted the demands of the Democrats, and I was again angry.

It was hard to keep track of American involvement in other countries and becoming harder all the time. Many things were started during Reagan's years as President that needed to be continued or finished with Bush in office. We had allowed America to be center stage with just about every foreign entity, a far cry from the old America before WWII. In 1989, just after the fall of the Berlin Wall, Bush met with Soviet General Secretary Mikhail Gorbachev in a conference on the Mediterranean island of Malta. The administration had been under intense pressure to meet with the Soviets, but not all initially found the Malta Summit to be a step in the right direction. General Brent Scowcroft, among others, was apprehensive about the meeting, saying that it might be "premature" due to concerns where, according to Condoleezza Rice, "expectations would be set that something was going to happen, where the Soviets might grandstand and force the U.S. into agreements that would ultimately not be good for the United States." But European leaders, including François Mitterrand and Margaret Thatcher, encouraged Bush to meet with Gorbachev, something that he did December 2 and 3, 1989.

In the 1980s, Panamanian leader Manuel Noriega, a

once U.S.-supportive leader who was later accused of spying for Fidel Castro and using Panama to traffic drugs into the United States, was one of the most recognizable names in America and was constantly in the press. The struggle to remove him from power began in the Reagan administration, when economic sanctions were imposed on the country. This included prohibiting American companies and the overnment from making payments to Panama and freezing $56 million in Panamanian funds in American banks. Reagan sent more than 2,000 American troops to Panama.

In May 1989, Panama held democratic elections, in which Guillermo Endara was elected president. The results were then annulled by Noriega's government. In response, Bush sent 2,000 more troops to the country, where they began conducting regular military exercises in Panamanian territory in violation of prior treaties. Bush then removed an embassy and ambassador from the country, and dispatched additional troops to Panama to prepare the way for an upcoming invasion. Noriega suppressed an October military coup attempt and massive protests in Panama against him, but after a U.S. serviceman was shot by Panamanian forces in

December 1989, Bush ordered 24,000 troops into the country with an objective of removing Noriega from power. "Operation Just Cause" was a large-scale American military operation, and the first in more than 40 years that was not related to the Cold War.

The mission was controversial, but American forces achieved control of the country and Endara assumed the Presidency. Americans did not like war, but the Panama invasion was justified by the shooting of an American soldier.

I hoped that Panama invasion would be the last of any more hostilities and Bush would get back to strengthening the economy. The stock market was showing signs of inflation fears, unemployment was back up because of failing businesses and the Democrat-driven tax increases were affecting everyone's bottom lines.

Then, on August 2, 1990, Iraq, led by Saddam Hussein, invaded its oil-rich neighbor to the south, Kuwait. Constant news stories and pictures of Iraqi forces storming buildings were unnerving to most, and intuitively frightening to me.

Bush condemned the invasion and began rallying opposition to Iraq in the US and among European, Asian, and Middle Eastern allies. Secretary of Defense "Dick" Cheney traveled to Saudi Arabia to meet with King Fahd. Fahd requested US military aid in the matter, fearing a possible invasion of his country as well. That was when I realized how in bed we were with Saudi Arabia. The request was met initially with Air Force fighter jets. Iraq made attempts to negotiate a deal that would allow the country to take control of half of Kuwait, Bush rejected this proposal and insisted on a complete withdrawal of Iraqi forces.

The planning of a ground operation by US-led coalition forces began forming in September 1990, headed by General Norman Schwarzkopf. Bush spoke before a joint session of the U.S. Congress regarding the authorization of air and land attacks, laying out four immediate objectives. "Iraq must withdraw from Kuwait completely, immediately, and without condition. Kuwait's legitimate government must be restored. The security and stability of the Persian Gulf must be assured. And American citizens abroad must be protected." He then outlined a fifth, long-term objective: "Out of these troubled times, our fifth objective, a new world order can emerge. A new era, freer from the threat of terror, stronger in the pursuit of justice, and more secure in the quest for peace. An era in which the nations of the world, East and West, North and South, can prosper and live in harmony. A world where the rule of law supplants the rule of the jungle. A world in which nations recognize the shared responsibility for freedom and justice. A world where the strong respect the rights of the weak."

With the United Nations Security Council opposed to Iraq's violence, Congress authorized the use of Military force with a set goal of returning control of Kuwait to the Kuwaiti government, and protecting America's interests abroad. The main interest was Saudi Arabia.

Bush met with Robert Gates, General Colin Powell, Secretary Dick Cheney, and others about the situation in the Persian Gulf and Operation Desert Shield, 15 January 1991

Early on the morning of January 17, 1991, allied forces launched the first attack, which included more than 4,000 bombing runs by coalition aircraft. This pace would continue for the next four weeks, until a ground invasion was launched on February 24, 1991. Allied forces penetrated Iraqi lines and pushed toward

Kuwait City, while on the west side of the country, forces were intercepting the retreating Iraqi army. Bush made the decision to stop the offensive after a mere 100 hours. Critics labeled this decision premature, as hundreds of Iraqi forces were able to escape, Bush responded by saying that he wanted to minimize U.S. casualties. Opponents further charged that Bush should have continued the attack, pushing Hussein's army back to Baghdad, then removing him from power. Bush explained that he did not give the order to overthrow the Iraqi government because it would have "incurred incalculable human and political costs. We would have been forced to occupy Baghdad and, in effect, rule Iraq."

Bush's approval ratings skyrocketed after the successful offensive. Additionally, President Bush and Secretary of State Baker, felt the coalition victory had increased U.S. prestige abroad and believed there was a window of opportunity to use the political capital generated by the coalition victory to revitalize the Arab-Israeli peace process.

I didn't trust anyone from the Middle East. Even though I was raised in a small town in Western New York, I had come in contact with Saudi Arabians several times as they surveyed possible land purchases and studied American culture. I knew oil was the reason for the preferred nation status of Saudi Arabia, but I didn't agree with it, and I didn't like it.

America had essentially helped them to find oil, sent our contractors there to drill and teach the Saudis how to find and cultivate their oil kingdom. Through essentially poor negotiations, America ended up with the short end of the stick, and oil from the Middle East was becoming our only resource for fuel. The Saudis started their own oil company while American oil reserves were becoming lower and lower. Rather than push for a better agreement where the Saudis took a low percentage of profits from the wells that we drilled and maintained, we instead got the small share and also had to pay rental and leasing fees. The return on our investment was the ability to build military bases on Saudi land, which gave us easier access to Russia and other potential enemies, but we also had to pay rent for those facilities, and promise to protect Saudi Arabia from its enemies.

So, we went to Kuwait and within 100 hours, Americans got to see thousands of Iraqis surrendering, their hands high in the air. Bush's popularity skyrocketed. Americans love to win. Not many understood why we went there, why we didn't go after Saddam Hussein, or what it would mean for the future, but we had lost in Viet Nam many years ago, and we needed heroes and needed to feel like winners.

We didn't have heroes like ones I had growing up. Mighty Mouse and Rocky Raccoon weren't realistic, but Superman was a household name and a "real" person, in our eyes anyway. We'd rush home to be sure we were done with chores and homework so we could watch the adventures of Superman and proudly echo his reason for being: "Truth, Justice, and the American way."

The white hat cowboys were a thing of the past, the Joker became more popular than Lois Lane and Clark Kent, and media of all kinds ranked up the ladder of importance. When I was 5, family, school, church, work, sports, and news were the priorities, but now television, computers, news, sports, school, work, family and church were the way to live, with television quickly losing ground to anything digital.

I tried to keep my kids away from As much of it as I could.   As toddlers, they watched old VCR tapes of

Disney movies, the Elephant show, and I Love Lucy. Sesame Street was not popular because Cookie Monster was still a monster.

When they got older, Music Television was the popular show, but there was no MTV at our house. They didn't need to hear lyrics that promoted violence or glorified sex.

As teenagers, I would catch them watching Jerry Springer or other so-called reality talk shows, and we'd have to have long conversations about people playing victims and the reasons they would even be on those shows.

Of course, I didn't realize until I was older that Leave it to Beaver and Father Knows Best were also not truthful or reality, but at least they portrayed family values that we wished for, and heroes within the family we could look up to. They were honest, responsible, and accountable, with a work ethic and a commitment to family. I wanted my kids to have a chance at those same values.

The quick war in Kuwait didn't really enforce those values, but it did restore some pride in being American, in our military, our ability to win, and that was okay with me.

The economy was still struggling, and I was also. American Express purchased IDS and began enforcing the use of their proprietary products. I didn't believe in that approach to anyone's finances. I believed in finding the product that fit the plan versus pushing the product to build the plan. Though I could have made higher commissions, I left IDS and went independent.

I was totally engrossed in succeeding and also in the education of my kids, so I was surprised when a client informed me about Bush's new plan. He was an officer in the AFL-CIO and his district was upset with Bush's plan to restructure tariffs and trade with Mexico and Canada. The North American Free Trade Agreement was not popular with unions who forecast ballooning trade deficits and the loss of jobs.

Bush spent the rest of his presidency trying to get NAFTA through congress, but failed.

Bush began his reelection campaign believing the Kuwait war victory would help him to win, but, ironically, the fall of the Soviet Union, the relatively peaceful Middle East, and the victory in

Kuwait, made the economy more important and Bush's rival for the Presidency pounced on that theme for his campaign.

Because the economy was so vital and America was again in a recession, a third candidate for the presidency emerged, Ross Perot.

Bill Clinton was the governor from Arkansas and I didn't have to do much work to determine my dislike for him. Though information was hard to get, there was just too much mystery around his governorship, too many plausible scandals, and he was not a President I wanted to see.

During the campaign, Arkansas first lady, Hillary Clinton's work for Little Rock's politically-connected Rose Law Firm erupted with suggestions of conflicts of interest regarding state business. The campaign dismissed the charge, but Bill Clinton elevated the importance of his lawyer-wife when he said that America would be getting "two for the price of one."

Hillary immediately had her thesis paper sealed, a thesis that glorified Saul Alinsky and his Rules For Radicals dedicated to Lucifer.

Bush had destroyed my belief that any two party system still existed, and the Clinton's long list of scandals and corruption while in Arkansas made me look closely at Ross Perot as a strong possibility.

Perot was a businessman who believed we needed someone with business acumen to turn our economy around. He also believed a strong economy would bring America back to its leadership role and provide the necessary revenues to keep the military strong and our borders safe.

I had never been active in politics before, but I took a stand and became a Perot supporter.

His headquarters in Buffalo was in the basement of a print shop, a damp, dark place now filled with banners, posters and signs. The owner told me it was the space he could use, but I could tell he was afraid to make it too obvious.

Many people were afraid to say they were Perot supporters, as if it was un-American to want someone the party bosses didn't want.

I manned my post diligently, day after day and night after night. People came with questions, doubts, fears of either Clinton or Bush retaliation. They knew about Whitewater. They knew about the women who claimed Bill Clinton had raped them. They knew Hillary as a shyster lawyer, and they didn't like her.

For the first time in my life, I posted a political sign in front of my home. The very next day, my car was splattered with paint and the sign torn to shreds. Bush supporters would never have done that. In fact, the problem with conservatives is that they're often too conservative.

Then, just like that, Perot dropped out of the race. His family had been threatened and he felt he had no choice. Again, it wasn't Bush who threatened him. Bush was the incumbent, almost a shoo in, and as marred as he was for caving to Democrats, he didn't have a public record of scandals and mysterious deaths.

The Clintons lived in one of the most corrupt cities in America, next to Chicago. Gangsters came there to avoid the law. Gambling, though illegal, was as out in the open as in Vegas. Theirs was the town of the black hat cowboys. There is evidence that many syndicate groups became involved in Hot Springs. Owney Madden was the overseer of everything and watched out for the New York mob's interests. Morris Kleinman, who was one of the founding gangsters of the Cleveland syndicate, spent much time in Hot Springs. It is rumored that the Cleveland boys had pieces of the profits from Hot Springs gambling. Johnny Roselli, an "upper level" member of the Chicago mob, was a silent partner in many Hot Springs casinos in the 1940's and 1950's, as was Frank Costello. All of these groups used local operators as "fronts", a system perfected by the Cleveland syndicate in Ohio, Florida, and Kentucky. Since Hot Springs was a very popular tourist spot, the command went out from the different syndicates that there should be no murders carried out in Hot Springs. This would be the rule in Las Vegas too. If bodies littered the streets like in Chicago, it would only hurt business. Also "petty" crimes like burglary and armed robbery were not to be tolerated. If the suckers weren't comfortable, they wouldn't come to Hot Springs.

Owney Madden laid the groundwork for gangsters on the lam to hide out in Hot Springs. The city had a resort-like atmosphere and elegant nightlife, with people coming and going all the time. This was the perfect situation to "hide" mobsters who couldn't be seen in their hometowns. Al Capone would stay at the Arlington Hotel when things got too hot in Chicago.

Clinton went to Georgetown University where he found a mentor in Professor Carroll Quigley. Quigley writes: "That the two political parties should represent opposed ideals and policies. . . is a foolish idea. Instead, the two parties should be almost identical . .The policies that are vital and necessary for America are no longer subjects of significant disagreement, but are disputable only in detail, procedure, priority, or method. "

The Clintons bought land in the Ozarks for $203,000 with mostly borrowed funds. The Clintons got 50% interest with no cash down. The 203 acre plot, known as Whitewater, is fifty miles from the nearest grocery store. The Washington Post reported that some purchasers of lots, many of them retirees, "put up houses or cabins, others slept in vans or tents, hoping to be able to live off the land." More than half of the purchasers lost their plots, thanks to the sleazy form of financing used.

Two months after commencing the Whitewater scam, Hillary Clinton invested $1,000 in cattle futures. Within a few days she had a $5,000 profit. Before bailing out, she earned nearly $100,000 on her investment. I knew what kind of investments these were and they were beyond high risk. The odds of Hillary making that kind of return on her short investment had to be a million to one.

As I learned more about the Clintons, I began to weep for my nation.

Ross Perot eventually came back to the campaign, but the massive amounts of money generated by the Clinton mobs overshadowed Bush, and Perot's votes did no damage. William Jefferson Clinton was elected president without question.

CHAPTER 7

One of the first things Clinton went to work on was completing the NAFTA agreement Bush had started. This free trade agreement between the United States, Canada and Mexico was supported by those who believed it would increase commerce between the countries by removing tariffs and other hindrances. Those against it, especially the unions, believed it would take away jobs and decrease American wages. Side deals for environmentalists and others had to be made before Congress would bring it to the table.

Meanwhile, Hillary Clinton went to work on what would be called Hillarycare, a socialist healthcare system leading to single payer healthcare that was touted as more fair to the poor. Hospitals were already mandated to see and receive anyone who came through their doors, and the poor were covered by Medicaid as the elderly were covered by Medicare.

We had the most efficient healthcare system in the world, the only flaw being the exorbitant costs, some of which was due to pharmaceutical and insurance companies competing for the most dollars from the consumer.

Doctors and hospital administrators were also at fault with hospital stays being charged to insurance companies and doctors raising their fees to cover malpractice injury lawsuits.

Hillarycare was a disaster from the beginning. Her advisors were globalists and socialists within both parties, and the Council on Foreign Affairs.

Ads were everywhere on television, and opinion pieces in major newspapers were extremely critical of the plan. In The Washington Post, conservative University of Virginia Professor Martha Derthick said, "In many years of studying American social policy, I have never read an official document that seemed so suffused with coercion and political naiveté, with its drastic prescriptions for controlling the conduct of state governments, employers, drug anufacturers, doctors, hospitals and you and me."

It was socialized medicine, and no one, not even many Democrats, were in agreement.

Luckily, mid-term elections returned a Republican majority to congress, and Hillary's bill would have to wait.

Meanwhile, Bill Clinton was emerged in countless foreign conflicts. Kosovo, Palestine and Israel, Iran, and Iraq. Iraq was amassing weapons of mass destruction and had in fact used mustard gas on the Kurds in the North. Clinton had launched missile strikes in Yugoslavia and Bosnia, but with Iraq, chose to amass troops at Iraq's border to Kuwait in a show of force. Remembering Bush's superiority in the previous Gulf war, the Iraqis backed away.

Clinton's biggest passion was the continued crisis between Palestine and Israel. He fostered two different peace plans between the warring factions, but when violence erupted once again, Netanyahu of Israel refused to give any more land to Palestine. He was subsequently removed from office, but would return a few years later.

It was hard to wrap my mind around all of the bombings and meetings and treaties. When it came to the Middle East, nothing was secure, and no one could be trusted.

One day, Clinton was sending money to Iran. The next he was bombing aspirin factories. He was sending troops in many directions and holding peace talks with unlikely allies.

His foreign policy was failing, but because Alan Greenspan was taking care of business with the economy, Americans weren't very interested in Iran, Iraq or the Saudi involvement in any of it.

Clinton faced yet another foreign crisis in early 1995, when the value of the Mexican peso began to fall sharply and threatened the collapse of the Mexican economy. Clinton believed the collapse of Mexico's economy would have a negative impact on the United States because of their close economic ties. He proposed a plan to address the financial crisis in Mexico, but many in Congress, fearing that constituents would not favor aid money to Mexico, rejected the plan. In response, Clinton drafted a $20 billion loan package for Mexico to restore international confidence in the Mexican economy. The loan was approved and Mexico completed its loan payments to the United States in January 1997, three years ahead of schedule. However, issues such as drug smuggling and U.S. immigration policies continued to strain relations between the United States and Mexico.

I traveled to San Diego, California on business, and also met one of my sons there for a day. He was a Marine MP, bilingual in Spanish, and would soon be a proud father.

He told me what was happening at the border between Mexico and California, things most Americans still knew nothing about. Any news about the border was usually from Arizona, for whatever reason, so even I was in the dark about California.

I had been stationed in San Diego, and at Camp Pendleton further north, for my four years in the Marines. I knew there were constant arrests and detainments, but that was over twenty years ago. I also knew Democrats had increased the number of allowed immigrants, a tactic to get more voters, and that many who got visas disappeared when their visas expired.

Nathan told me about tunnels, tunnel cities, large weapons and military grade weapons, all being transported along with massive amounts of cocaine and other drugs.

He said when Reagan was in office, the borders seemed more secure, but since Bush, and now with Clinton, they were much more porous. His border patrol friends were becoming more and more frustrated at lack of funding and lack of personnel, and that he and other MPs often caught dozens of illegals crossing over military land, only to see the same people back again in only weeks.

I told him we used to go to Mexico all the time, and when I was stationed there, Tijuana was a short walk away. The poverty was obvious, but we also went to other parts of Mexico on vacation and their economy seemed to be booming.

"Drugs," he said. "It's the drug cartels. They bribe anyone they can use so they get their drugs on the highways. We now have a crossover in New Mexico where the police wait for a call so they can escort the drug lords over the border to safety. They make an extra $50,000 a year and think nothing of what they're doing to the country."

"I don't know what to tell you," I said. "I think our government has turned in a direction that's not American any more. Democrats open our borders. Republicans become Democrats. Everyone lies. Everyone is on the take. I'm sure most of them are in on the drug deals because they get richer and richer even when the economy is killing you and me."

That's not all," he said. "They're selling girls. Sex slaves. Mexicans, Americans, Asians, they're kidnapping and selling them. And word has it, it's not just Congress, but all the way to the top. I wanna do something about it, but I don't know what to do."

"I don't get it. Clinton is locking everybody up, you know, that three strikes you're out legislation. I think he's also continuing Reagan's war on drugs. He doesn't talk about immigration very much, but he's a democrat and they always want more voters. I just don't know. In the old days we would march on Washington, but there's really no organizing issue, not yet, anyway."

He sighed, checked his watch and had to leave.

"Jan's having a girl," he said. "I don't want this stuff happening and affecting my little girl."

I got back to New York just in time to see the news about a bombing at the World Trade Center. A truck bomb had exploded in the garage killing 6 people, and the smoke coupled with poor evacuation guidelines, caused more than one thousand injuries.

Ramzi Yousef was one of the bombers. Born in Kuwait, he was living in Pakistan and arrived in New York City illegally. He was given a court date, then wandered around the city until it was time to make his bomb.

Clinton's televised reaction infuriated me and many others. He treated it like a crime investigation, told people to calm down, and said whoever did it would be brought to justice. He was disengaged, busy with other things on his mind, and he would be that way for every terrorist attack that happened on his watch.

Clinton's scandals and foreign policy ineptitude began piling up. In late May, independent counsel Kenneth Starr had convicted Jim and Susan McDougal and Jim Guy Tucker in the first big Whitewater trial. In June, the Filegate story first broke into public view, and Sen. Alphonse D'Amato issued his committee's Whitewater report recommending that several administration officials be investigated for perjury. It was also in June that the White House went into full battle mode against a variety of allegations contained in Unlimited Access, a book by former FBI agent, Gary Aldrich.

The last act of terrorism during the Clinton administration came on October 12, 2000, when bin Laden operatives bombed the USS Cole in Aden, Yemen. Seventeen American sailors were killed, 39 others were wounded, and one of the U.S.'s most sophisticated warships was nearly sunk. Clinton's reaction to the Cole terrorism was more muted than his response to the previous attacks. While he called the bombing "a despicable and cowardly act" and said, "We will find out who was responsible and hold them accountable," he seemed more concerned that the attack might threaten the administration's work in the Middle East. In September, 1993, officials on both sides announced that they had been in contact with one another, and they shared details about their meetings. Reaction on both sides was mixed. At this point, the accords had not yet been formally ratified.

On September 10, 1993, Clinton announced that the Oslo Accords would be formalized in a ceremony on the White House lawn three days later. Warren Christopher, the Secretary of State in the Clinton administration, had been instrumental in keeping the Oslo talks on track.

Clinton personally tried to persuade Israeli Prime Minister Yitzhak Rabin and PLO Chairman Yasser Arafat to attend. He felt that the image of old foes Rabin and Arafat making peace would be of incalculable worth to the peace process.

Clinton encouraged the two former adversaries to shake hands. While Arafat was willing, Rabin was initially reluctant. In his memoir, My Life, Clinton recalled how Rabin finally agreed to shake hands, saying, "I suppose that one does not make peace with one's friends."

By the year 2000, Clinton attempted to resurrect the peace talks. One of the conditions of the Oslo Accords was that agreement on all outstanding issues should be reached within five years. This agreement would be the penultimate step to Palestinian autonomy in the Gaza Strip and West Bank. While a number of contentious issues remained, perhaps the most significant issue concerned the status of Jerusalem. The Palestinians wanted control of East Jerusalem, home to several sites considered holy by both Jews and Muslims. Israel was willing to grant Palestinians custody of some holy sites, but wanted to maintain sovereignty over Jerusalem.

Despite days of presidential cajoling and arm bending, the 2000 Camp David Summit was inconclusive. President Clinton, for his part, assigned much of the blame to Yasser Arafat. He felt that Israeli Prime Minister Ehud Barak had made a reasonable offer. Barak endorsed the idea of East Jerusalem serving as the capital of the Palestinian territories, though he still balked at the suggestion of

Israel turning over sovereignty of any part of Jerusalem. Arafat did not respond to Barak's proposal, he simply walked away. The fact that the Second Intifada began shortly after the 2000 Camp David Summit broke down suggested that Arafat and the PLO were no longer interested in making peace, they were simply hoping to extract concessions from the Israeli government.

The Clinton's were finally getting ready to leave office and I was more than ready for that to happen. Bill had dishonored the Oval Office with his sexual infidelity, lied about it, committed perjury, was impeached, but stayed in office until the end. His wife not only accepted what he had done, but when more women came forward to expose his capers with them while in office, she used her power to destroy their credibility and smear their names. Her attacks were straight from the Saul Alinsky handbook,"Rules For Radicals." Hillary idolized Alinsky, wrote her thesis about him, and sealed her thesis as soon she entered politics.

The Alinsky theme was based on isolating the "enemy" and destroying that enemy using collective actions. "Power is not only what you have, but what the enemy thinks you have." Power is derived from 2 main sources, money and people. "Have-Nots" must build power from flesh and blood.

1. "Never go outside the expertise of your people." It results in confusion, fear and retreat. Feeling secure adds to the backbone of anyone.

2. "Whenever possible, go outside the expertise of the enemy." Look for ways to increase insecurity, anxiety and uncertainty.

3. "Make the enemy live up to its own book of rules." If the rule is that every letter gets a reply, send 30,000 letters. You can kill them with this because no one can possibly obey all of their own rules.

4. "Ridicule is man's most potent weapon." There is no defense. It's irrational. It's infuriating. It also works as a key pressure point to force the enemy into concessions.

5. "A good tactic is one your people enjoy." They'll keep doing it without urging and come back to do more. They're doing their thing, and will even suggest better ones.

6. "A tactic that drags on too long becomes a drag." Don't become old news.

7. "Keep the pressure on. Never let up." Keep trying new things to keep the opposition off balance. As the opposition masters one approach, hit them from the flank with something new.

8. "The threat is usually more terrifying than the thing itself." Imagination and ego can dream up many more consequences than any activist.

9. "The major premise for tactics is the development of operations that will maintain a constant pressure upon the opposition." It is this unceasing pressure that results in the reactions from the opposition that are essential for the success of the campaign.

10. "If you push a negative hard enough, it will push through and become a positive." Violence from the other side can win the public to your side because the public sympathizes with the underdog.

11. "The price of a successful attack is a constructive alternative." Never let the enemy score points because you're caught without a solution to the problem.

12. "Pick the target, freeze it, personalize it, and polarize it." Cut off the support network and isolate the target from sympathy. Go after people and not institutions; people hurt faster than institutions.

Hillary used number 13 to gain support for her upcoming run for Senator from the state of New York. She also used her gender constantly, something that is demeaning to women, but many women fell into the same victim energy and felt compelled to vote for gender. She was touted as "the smartest woman in the world," a brand that would stick with her throughout the rest of her career.

CHAPTER 8

I was much more involved and awake to the upcoming presidential election, but I was also in the midst of a move from liberal New York to conservative Alabama. New York State under the democrats had Buffalo nearing record poverty levels and the industries surrounding Buffalo shutting down or moving to Mexico. Clinton's NAFTA agreement affected the unions and wages and many in the city were forced to move elsewhere.

I was now more entrepreneurial and independent, something I often encouraged others to pursue. After all, part of the "American Dream," was to become as successful as you wanted to be or could be doing what you love to do. In fact, unless you love what you do, success can be very difficult.

I didn't know the politics of Alabama at all, and I had stereotypes of what life in the South was all about. I also didn't know how absolutely beautiful Alabama was until I gave a few talks and speeches and got to see that the stereotypes were all wrong.

Al Gore was Clinton's Vice President, and as is custom, began his run for the presidency in the primaries. George W. Bush, the son of Bush senior and the governor of Texas, also announced his run for that office.

I couldn't believe America would have to deal with another Bush, but I also knew enough about Gore to begin informing others why they shouldn't vote for him.

The Bush campaign focused mainly on domestic issues, such as the projected budget surplus, proposed reforms of Social Security and Medicare, health care, and competing plans for tax relief. Foreign policy was a big issue, and Bush criticized Clinton administration policies in Somalia, where 18 Americans died in 1993 trying to sort out warring factions, and in the Balkans, where United States peacekeeping troops perform a variety of functions.

"I don't think our troops ought to be used for what's called nation building," Bush said in the second presidential debate. Bush also pledged to bridge partisan gaps in the nation's capital, claiming the atmosphere in Washington stood in the way of progress on necessary reforms.

Gore, meanwhile, questioned Bush's fitness for the job, pointing to gaffes made by Bush in interviews and speeches, and suggesting the Texas governor lacked the necessary experience to be president. It seemed every Democrat running for office always began with stating his or her opponent lacked the necessary experience.

Bill Clinton's impeachment, and the sex scandal that led up to it, cast a shadow on the campaign, particularly on his vice president's run to replace him. Republicans strongly denounced the Clinton scandals, particularly Bush, who made his repeated promise to restore "honor and dignity" to the White House a centerpiece of his campaign.

Gore studiously avoided the Clinton scandals, as did Lieberman, even though Lieberman had been the first Democratic senator to denounce Clinton's misbehavior. In fact, some media observers theorized that Gore actually chose Lieberman for his Vice President in an attempt to separate himself from Clinton's past misdeeds, and help blunt the GOP's attempts to link him to his boss. Others pointed to the passionate kiss Gore gave his wife during the Democratic Convention, as a signal that despite the allegations against Clinton, Gore himself was a faithful husband.

When Gore came to Buffalo before I left for Alabama, I hated that all I heard from my many clients was how good looking he was or how well he spoke. It seemed to me that we were slowly transforming to a nation that only cared about looks and speech, not character or content. That was a negative for Bush, as he often misspoke and was the brunt of many jokes about his intellectual capabilities.

Bush's platform included promising a humble foreign policy with no nation building. He had criticized the Clinton-Gore Administration for being too interventionist. "If we don't stop extending our troops all around the world in nation-building missions, then we're going to have a serious problem coming down the road. And I'm going to prevent that."

On the economy, Bush promised tax breaks for all, sometimes using the slogan "Whoever pays taxes gets a tax break." The rich pay the most taxes, and the current system weighs the income tax against the upper income brackets. Bush also supported raising the Earned Income Tax Credit, which would primarily benefit the lower brackets of income-tax-affected citizens.

He proposed the No Child Left Behind premise for education which would increase funding for schools based on results. That premise was pushing the education of our children further into federal government control.

Gore's plan for education was similar in that the federal government would gain more and more control. He extended his platform to include funding pre-school and making sure every classroom had internet. He at one point even said he invented the internet, which everyone knew wasn't true.

The main thing that people needed to know about Gore was his membership in the Club of Rome. The Club of Rome, a global think tank that uses almost any means possible to effect globalization, population reduction, and what we know as the New World Order.

So our choices for the year 2000 were a Bush whose father was ex-CIA and a New World Order promoter as President, and a Clinton Vice President who belonged to a powerful club that embarked on using what they themselves called a false science of climate change to achieve basically the same results. Either one would lead America closer to the U.N. Agenda 21, which eventually could lead to America's loss of sovereignty under the U.N.

It's no wonder this was one of the closest elections in history and had to be decided by the Supreme Court. Voters had no choice at all except name recognition and a Vice President.

The Supreme Court prevailed for Bush in a 5-4 vote, and America now referred to him as Bush '43 to distinguish him from his father, Bush '41.

I didn't pay much attention to Bush in the first months of his presidency. He was pushing and implementing some of his campaign promises around education, healthcare, and doing what I agreed with regarding climate change by withdrawing from the Kyoto protocol on world climate change. I didn't trust his foreign policy, especially since his V.P. was Dick Cheney. Cheney was Bush senior's Secretary of Defense, and he maintained ties with Halliburton, a company with global interests in oil.

On September 11, 2001, I did something I never do. I felt I should turn on the news for whatever reason, and kept it on a news program while I worked on other things. When I heard the newscaster say it looked like a plane hit the world trade center, my instantaneous response was "They've come back." I knew immediately it was terrorism, most likely Bin Laden or the Al Queda group from Afghanistan, and I immediately began packing for a trip back to New York.

Before I had finished a quick suitcase pack, the second plane hit tower 2 and the pundits on television began figuring out that this was an attack.

I packed the car, had a friend get me whatever American flag she could find, and watched the towers burn until they collapsed. Within minutes of the collapse, I had draped a very large flag over the trunk of my car and was on the road to the Big Apple.

News reports were constant. Another plane hit the Pentagon. Bush was in the air. Cheney was in the bunker in D.C. Another plane crashed in Pennsylvania. I was as dazed, angry and upset as I knew people in the city were. I had many friends in the towers from my years in the financial services industry, and I prayed for them, hoping they had escaped or would be found alive.

When I stopped for gas somewhere in Kentucky, I was amazed at how apathetic people were to what had happened. They saw it as just another attack in New York, a city that had nothing to with them. The Pentagon? Well, that was Washington, D.C. and they were the cause of all of this to begin with.

The truckers were angry. The fire departments were already on their way to help. The police were apprehensive about where the next attack might be. But the people, the store workers, the tourists ending their vacations, were amazingly detached from it all, some even looking at me as if I was crazy to be so upset. I arrived at night and all roads in and out of the city were closed. I could smell and see the acrid smoke from New Jersey as I parked and tried to find a ferry or boat that could take me to the piers. When I finally got to the piers, I almost froze at what I saw. The devastation was so immense and widespread that television cameras couldn't come close to showing the reality.

Photos of those missing were already covering the fences and poles. People of all colors, shapes and sizes were walking and pacing in a daze, some covered with ash or soot, others brandishing cuts and blood, all as clueless on what to do next as I was.

Time stood still, and also sped by in a flash. Fireman were returning to the scene to look for survivors, and though I tried to join them, Mayor Guliani had already begun to control the scene by allowing only those with experience or affiliated first responders to attempt any rescue. I, instead, used my experience as a counselor and therapist from mynattive teachings to do what I could for those traumatized, bewildered, or lost.

I spent 2 days and nights on the streets comforting, listening, and even caring for rescue dogs and cats who were frustrated and burned as they searched for anyone they could find to please their masters. I carried a battered, now parentless child, to a policeman. Her mother crushed by a falling body and her father trapped in the imploded tower. I decided then that I should make my way to Buffalo. My kids and friends were there, and I had a rescue dog without an owner who needed care for her paws and her grief.

One of the first things I did when I got to Buffalo was to drive by the Peace Bridge and the water treatment facilities. There was no special security at either place and that bothered me. I went to the Junior High School to pick up my youngest and she was relieved I was there. She said kids were scared and she was sure terrorists were close by. I tried to reassure her they weren't close and that the President would take care of things so she shouldn't be scared, but when we went to a copy store so she could finish a homework assignment, she came out running to the car in a panic.

"There's a man in there copying driver's licenses and passport papers," she whispered. Her whisper was more like a silent scream and her pale, frightened face told me her observation was real. I caught a glimpse of the man through the window and was more convinced there was a problem. He was dressed in the Muslim garb I had grown accustomed to seeing at the University and in town, bearded, tall, and very determined. We went to her favorite restaurant so she could eat and calm down, and I called the local FBI office to tell them what we saw. They laughed at me. They said there were no terrorists in the area and I needed to "get a grip" on myself. When I told them about the water plants on the south side of town, they laughed again, told me to have a nice day, and hung up.

Two weeks later, a large terror cell with at least eleven Middle Eastern men was found less than 15 miles from downtown Buffalo.

President Bush addressed the nation and went to NYC to not only assess the damage, but to also support the responders and meet with the mayor. His bullhorn rang out that the people who did this would soon hear from America, and that American spirit that had disappeared after Pearl Harbor, came back with a vengeance with cries of "USA, USA, USA!

CHAPTER 9

It seemed to take forever for America to retaliate for 9/11, most people unsure what was being done, or if they were in NYC, were they safe? Mayor Guliani was both loved and hated for his tenure as mayor, but as the days continued with some survivors and hundreds of victims, his daily briefings, often wracked with emotion, kept America informed and vigilant.

President Bush's first policy response to 9/11 came on October 8, 2001, when during a speech to Congress, he announced the creation of the Office of Homeland Security, and appointed Tom Ridge, a former governor of Pennsylvania, as its director. This was the first new executive-level office to be created since 1988, when President Ronald Reagan had appointed a head of the Department of Veterans Affairs. The stated purpose of the Office of Homeland Security was "to develop and coordinate the implementation of a comprehensive national strategy" and "to secure the United States from terrorist threats or attacks."

Following the terrorist attacks of September 11, 2001, the Taliban had described Osama Bin Laden as their guest, and refused to place him in United States custody, although Bin Laden may have been hiding out of the reach of the Taliban, in the mountains of Afghanistan. The U.S.-led invasion of Afghanistan overthrew the Taliban from the capital Kabul, and from large areas of Afghanistan, and a U.S.-approved government was installed. The majority of Al-Qaeda members, including Osama Bin Laden, were not captured.

That's when I started questioning the 9/11 attacks. I watched the videos over and over again and it seemed there were planes that hit the buildings, but my military and pilot friends told me they were not commercial planes.

So why would attack buildings in New York, the Pentagon and make a hole in the ground in Pennsylvania? The day before the attacks, Rumsfeld announced 2.8 trillion dollars was missing from the State Department. How convenient, I thought, that that story was now buried by the tower attacks.

And why did Guliani immediately ship any and all steel from the towers overeseas, leaving nothing to investigate possible explosives?

When I saw building 7 come down, an obvious implosion, I researched who and what was in that building. The CIA, Department of Defense, the FBI and money/gold.

We were all led to believe it was Bin Laden and Saudi Arabia who attacked, but now I questioned it. I wasn't part of the 9/11 truther movement, but I felt we needed many more answers.

Guantanamo Bay in Cuba was opened as a prison for "enemy combatants," many or all of them with ties to Al Queda, but also other terrorist groups. Bush was criticized for sending an insufficient number of troops into Afghanistan initially and thus failing to achieve all of the mission's objectives, but the Bush administration was successful in freezing Al-Qaeda funds and shutting down many of the terrorist training camps. The U.S. captured many Al-Qaeda leaders and members in the months and years following the invasion.

Bush's approval ratings following the invasion in Afghanistan were above 90%, the highest for any president since ratings began. His "Faith Based Initiative" extended to the troops who were able to copy the Presidents scripture quotes to their helmets or rifles seemed okay, but I did wonder if it was just a cover to make the war God versus Allah and secure American support.

In 2002, during his State of the Union Address, Bush set forth what has become known as the Bush Doctrine. Although this doctrine was technically used for justifying the invasion of Afghanistan, it was not clearly stated as a matter of policy until this address. Simply put, because of the "new world" Americans were now living in, and the possibility of further massive terrorist attacks orchestrated by organizations that existed in multiple places all over the world, the United States could no longer think of the world as being exclusively made up of sovereign nations. Because of this, the United States would now implement a policy of using preemptive military strikes against any nation known to be harboring or aiding a terrorist organization hostile to the United States.

Not only was he setting the precedent of nation building, something he campaigned against in opposition to Clinton, but it was obvious, to me anyway, that he had received guidance from his father, Bush '41, in using this crisis as a portal or gateway to the New World Order and global governance.

He also outlined what he called the Axis of Evil, consisting of three nations that he stated posed the greatest threat to world peace at the time. These were Iraq, North Korea and Iran.

His administration started pushing the narrative that officials had evidence for the development of weapons of mass destruction (WMDs) in Iraq. The description of these devices ranged from chemical weapons to nuclear warheads with their associated delivery systems. They supported this claim with intelligence documents as well as aerial photographs. Saddam Hussein, the President of Iraq, was described as being a threat to the world and to his own people as long as he remained in power, especially if his regime had access to WMDs. Saddam had been supplied with conventional weapons and other assistance by the United States during the Iran–Iraq War in the 1980s, but since then, the political arena had changed, especially due to an increasingly hardline stance taken by Saddam in Iraq, and his arbitrary invasion of Kuwait in 1990 which Bush's father curtailed.

The armed forces of the United States and several other countries invaded Iraq in 2003, on my birthday. The operation was known in the United States as Operation Iraqi Freedom. Although the American government, with encouragement from the British Prime Minister Tony Blair, had attempted to gain a United Nations Security Council resolution authorizing the use of force to remove Saddam from power, the attempt was unsuccessful. Proponents of the use of force pointed to current and previous violations by Iraq of resolutions and sanctions imposed by the United Nations and the UN Security Council, as substantive enough to justify military intervention.

President Bush, however, drew criticism for preemptively attacking a country that had never attacked the United States or threatened to do so, and for disregarding the opinion of the United Nations. He was criticized also, especially at home, for diverting attention away from capturing Osama Bin Laden. When asked during a press conference in March 2002 about what he was doing to capture Bin Laden, the president remarked: "You know, I just don't spend that much time on him."

On May 2, from the flight deck of the USS Abraham Lincoln, in front of a huge banner that read "Mission Accomplished," Bush declared that "major combat operations in Iraq have ended." This drew criticism for being premature, since many Coalition forces were still fighting in Iraq. The banner, some said, was supposed to have been removed before the speech, and the president had not been involved.

Following the U.S.-led invasion of Iraq, the Iraq Survey Group (ISG), made up of 1,200 members of British and American experts in the field of concealed weapons programs, was established. On October 3, 2003, it released its Interim report on Iraq, which stated that it had found numerous "WMD related materials" but no actual WMDs.

On November 27, 2003, the president made a surprise visit to Iraq to share a Thanksgiving dinner with the soldiers there in an effort to raise low morale. He spent two hours eating with troops at Baghdad International Airport before returning to the U.S. The visit was kept top secret, and even the army personnel had no idea he was coming. Some saw it as a patriotic gesture; others as a dangerous political stunt. Accompanied by U.S. National Security adviser Condoleezza Rice, the trip went without incident.

Bush spoke to the press during a meeting with congressional leaders in the Oval Office. Friday, March 21, 2003.

A few weeks later, on December 13, Saddam Hussein, the deposed President of Iraq, was found and captured by U.S. forces. Pictures of the now bearded former leader, looking severely dazed, being poked and prodded by medical examiners, circulated in newspapers and on the Internet around the world. Most Americans were pleased that Saddam had been found and captured.

I read many of the criticisms of Bush, especially all the controversy over whether Saddam had wmds, and I was torn. Bush had said from the onset of 9/11 that the United States would go to any country that was harboring or aiding terrorists and congress and the American people agreed with him. Iraq had used mustard gas to kill its own citizens, and used scud missiles against Israel where everyone wore gas masks in case Saddam used chemicals. I guess I was angry enough at the attack and the fact that if Clinton had done his job, we might not have been attacked at all, that I supported any action against Iraq and would also support going after Iran.

Bush ran against John Kerry for his second term, and Kerry was another one I knew well. He was considered a traitor by Viet Nam veterans and caught in numerous lies about his service and the honor of the servicemen who were

in Viet Nam. He even nominated himself for a purple heart

for a self-inflicted wound. He was a liar and a traitor so I had

no difficulty once again voting for Bush.

Bush prevailed by a narrow margin, a surprise to me, but

he thought his victory was a mandate to put forth his entire agenda.

I didn't see a mandate in such a close vote, and frankly, I was

growing very tired of the left versus the right that only divided a

wounded nation.

What had happened to the notion that we were the United

States and not red versus blue? Reagan had tried to stop the

division of Communist versus Capitalist by telling us his

election was the choice between America going up or down.

Bush's so-called mandate reminded me of why the

Founders had created a system of checks and balances so no

one individual could become the same as a King.

By the time Bush gave his State of the Union address in

2007, the mid-term elections had shown the American public's

disdain for Bush's mandates, and Bush lost the House and Senate

to Democrats. Nancy Pelosi became the first woman Speaker of the House and I knew we were now in worse trouble than ever before.

Pelosi's right-hand man was a Soros operative, and George Soros so hated George Bush that he proceeded to put millions of dollars into the next Presidential campaign in support of Hillary Clinton.

I immediately got to work researching her opponents on both sides, and I wasn't happy, I was enraged.

CHAPTER 10

When you look at John Kerry, Hillary Clinton, Pelosi, Barbara Boxer, and Hillary's new Democratic opponent, Barack Obama, you find one commonality that should alarm all Americans. They are and have been on the Soros payroll, and they have taken the money without a hint of conscience. One quote from George Soros should be enough to enrage every American.

"The main obstacle to a stable and just world order is the United States."

George Soros, György Schwartz, better known to the world as George Soros, was born August 12, 1930 in Hungary. Soros' father, Tivadar, was a fervent practitioner of the Esperanto, a language invented in 1887, and designed to be the first global language, free of any national identity.

He considers himself to be an elitist world class philosopher, despises the American Way, and just loves open borders and social engineering.

The Schwartz's, who were non-practicing Jews, changed the family name to Soros, in order to facilitate assimilation into the gentile population, as the Nazis spread into Hungary during the 1930s. When Hitler's henchman, Adolf Eichmann, arrived in Hungary to oversee the murder of that country's Jews, George Soros ended up with a man whose job was confiscating property from the Jewish population. Soros went with him on his rounds. 70% of Mr. Soros's fellow Jews in Hungary, nearly a half million human beings, were annihilated in that year.

After WWII, Soros attended the London School of Economics, where he fell under the thrall of fellow atheist and Hungarian, Karl Popper, one of his professors.

Popper was a mentor to Soros until Popper's death in 1994. Two of Popper's most influential teachings concerned "the open society," and Fallibilism, the latter being the belief that all claims of knowledge could, in principle, be mistaken.

By his own admission, he helped engineer coups in Slovakia, Croatia, Georgia, and Yugoslavia. When Soros targets a country for "regime change," he begins by creating a shadow government, a fully formed government-in-exile, ready to assume power when the opportunity arises. The Shadow Party he has built in America greatly resembles those he has created in other countries prior to instigating a coup.

By 2007, Soros almost completely owned the Democratic Party, and it was time for a full attack and regime change in Washington.

Pelosi was given the order to devote all of her time to ensuring a Democrat-led House and Senate by 2009, a mission she took on so steadfastly that she wasn't aware of waterboarding being used in the Gulf war and accused the State Department and CIA of lying to congress. Congress was routinely briefed on all aspects of the war, but Pelosi had set her sights on the upcoming presidential election and claimed otherwise.

Soros' main problem was which candidate should get the most backing and support for the presidency. Hillary was a favorite and could capture the women's vote that was now a hefty percentage of her support.

Obama was black, or at least, identified as Black, so he could capture the black vote easily, a necessary voting bloc for election. He knew Blacks would vote Democrat because they were told to do so, but women could easily change their minds, especially if they remembered the follies of Hillary's husband and her support of him.

John McCain on the Republican side was also close to Soros, and considered a Republican in name only by many. His choice of Sarah Palin as a running mate could also capture the women's vote along with the military and veteran vote.

It was all a chess game, a win-win for Soros no matter who ran or who won, America would be forever changed, and most likely well on its way to being a third world country with open borders and part of the New World Order.

Half way through the Democratic primary, Hillary and Obama disappeared for a few hours, and even their friendly press didn't know where they went.

Within three days after their mysterious meeting, Hillary began losing to Obama in key states, her poll numbers tanked, and she was out of the race. The Golden Boy for Soros would be Barack Hussein Obama. Just in case Hillary's female voters flocked to Sarah Palin to vote gender, Soros was covered, and the charade, façade, of an election could be carried out.

I had followed Obama since I saw his first book on Amazon, and since his keynote address at the Democratic convention. What I saw was a smooth operator, a man who could read teleprompters if the words weren't too difficult, and a liar. In interview after interview, he basically stated his agenda, but it was as if no one was listening. He said he'd "spread the wealth around," and that America had to be on a "level playing field" with everyone else.

I read his books, and I was convinced he didn't write them. What I did see in the books was an anti-colonialist who hated America and the British for colonizing South Africa, and for forming the United States even though it was British rule that caused the American Revolution.

The media from all sides was complicit in making him a rock star, fawning over the possibility of the first Black president.

Just as Hillary had done when she first entered politics in Arkansas, Obama sealed all of his records so people could only trace the past he wished to present.

"Who does that?" I asked my friends. "Who seals their records if they have nothing to hide?"

I became more and more enraged. I felt, maybe knew, that this was the final leg in the Progressive Coup D' Etat and so many Americans had no clue.

Then a few network people started doing some of the research themselves. They exposed Reverend Jerimiah Wright, Obama's pastor for 20 years, a man Obama trusted. Wright believed in Black Liberation theology, that the United States was inherently racist, and that America itself should succumb to Marxism.

Obama immediately distanced himself from Wright even though less than two weeks prior to Wright's exposure Obama had proclaimed his undying friendship and camaraderie.

Video appeared of Wright's sermons blasting his hatred of America, but Obama, the liar, said in twenty years of once-a-week sermons, he never once heard Wright speak like that. It was time for a distraction straight out of Alinsky's playbook. The media took aim at Sarah Palin. She became the enemy, and all the radical rules came into play to destroy her.

While Hillary was still in the running, she brought up the question of Obama's citizenship, the first one to question his birth certificate. Though I'm sure she was instructed not to do that, her quest for power would overshadow the party line as long as she could win. She opened that dialogue and many people who now had access to the internet started researching his birth.

Nancy Pelosi, as Speaker of the House, had to certify Obama's eligibility to run in each state. When the eligibility forms were scrutinized, it was found that there were two different forms used, one of them with no mention of citizenship to give Obama free rein to run.

Americans were hurting. The Iraq war was costing money, and Bush had run up deficits because Congress wouldn't okay extended spending. Bush had also asked several times for regulations to be placed on banks dealing with the housing market, but congress, the Democrats, assured him the housing market was fine. The Dodd-Frank bill allowed for paperless mortgages, a scheme to allow poorer people to purchase homes they really couldn't afford. When McCain started climbing in the polls, mostly because of Palin, it was time for the big distraction that would change America and destroy McCain.

Bush signed legislation that allowed the U.S. Treasury to put its proposed Troubled Asset Relief Program into effect. Treasury Secretary Hank Paulson told Congress its implementation was required to stem a worldwide economic collapse. Bush acted within hours of its passage by the House.

Formally called the Emergency Economic tabilization Act, the measure bailed out banks in the wake of the subprime mortgage debacle. It authorized the Treasury to spend as much as $700 billion in taxpayer funds to buy mortgage-backed securities and other distressed assets as a means of restoring confidence in badly shaken credit markets.

McCain felt he was needed back in Washington to help determine the right course of action, so he temporarily suspended his campaign while Obama continued his schedule. Obama was smug about McCains departure, stating numerous times that McCain couldn't multi-task like he could, and capitalizing on the fact that McCain really wasn't needed in Washington because everything had already been put in place.

By this time, I had learned social networking and was posting my antagonism toward both candidates on a regular basis. I disagreed with TARP and knew Bush had been played, but it was too late to do anything about it except complain to my representatives. I had to at least let them know their re-elections could be jeopardized by following Pelosi's lead.

On paper, the Emergency Economic Stabilization Act of 2008 was simple. The Treasury would buy $700 billion of troubled mortgages from the banks and then modify them to help struggling homeowners. Section 109 of the act, in fact, specifically empowered the Treasury secretary to "facilitate loan modifications to prevent avoidable foreclosures." With that promise on the table, Democrats finally approved the bailout "That provision," says Barofsky, "is what got the bill passed." But within days of passage, the Fed and the Treasury unilaterally decided to abandon the planned purchase of toxic assets in favor of direct injections of billions in cash into companies like Goldman and Citigroup. Overnight, Section 109 was unceremoniously ditched, and what was pitched as a bailout of both banks and homeowners instantly became a bank-only operation – marking the first in a long series of moves in which bailout officials either casually ignored, or openly defied their own promises with regard to TARP.

I and many others were furious that the government thought we were too stupid to understand what they were doing. We called, emailed, Tweeted, posted, even snail-mailed Washington to express our anger and tell them to stop the spending.

Voicemail boxes were full, email went unanswered, and the D.C. elite continued doing whatever was in their best interest.

Obama began pushing his healthcare agenda in his town halls and speeches, stating unequivocally that people could keep their doctors, their plans, and his healthcare bill would save people $2500 per year.

I knew his healthcare plan was really Hillarycare with additional tweaks, but my main focus was trying to stop his election any way I could. Granted, I was watching every news station and special program I could get my hands on just to get a handle on the range of problems with an Obama presidency. There was almost too much to handle.

On September 15, 2008, Lehman Brothers, one of the largest investment banks in the world, failed. Over the next few months, the US stock market plummeted, liquidity dried up, successful companies laid off employees by the thousands, and for the first time there was no longer any doubt that we were in a recession.

Of course, Bush was being blamed for all of it, when in fact it was the Democrats in Congress who refused regulations on the housing market and on banks, dating back to Clinton's time in office.

In 1993, the growth in the housing market was 63 percent. By the end of the Clinton administration, it was 68 percent. The growth in the Bush administration was about 1 percent.

As reported in various papers, including the New York Times, in 1999, Fannie Mae and Freddie Mac were under pressure from the Clinton administration to increase lending to minorities and low income home buyers, a policy that necessarily entailed higher risks. I knew where the reduced lending standards and boost in home ownership came from. I also knew why.

One only had to research Goldman-Sachs, which candidates were connected to them, and to remember George Soros' command to Hillary. There is no way that Hillary Clinton would back down to an Obama election without assured promises of both monetary gain, and political power. The gain began and would continue through a money-laundering scheme with the Clinton Foundation, and the power would be her appointment as Secretary of State as she waited in the wings for 2016.

CHAPTER 11

I did all I could do as a little person, a common American, but on election day, even though my own exit polling said people weren't voting for him, Obama won.

I went to my knees and wept for America. I then decided, maybe to set a good example for the kids around me, or maybe to make sure I wasn't right about Obama, to give him a chance. I stopped posting negative things, removed my many podcasts from Tunes, and hoped for the best. It only took three days to realize I had been more than right.

Besides asking for and getting more bailout money from Bush before Bush left office, Obama was promised an $850 billion dollar stimulus plan by early February, and a $35 billion dollar health plan for children being rushed through Congress. With Reid and Pelosi at the helms of both the house and the senate, Republicans barely had a chance.

I screamed out loud for all to hear, "Stop the spending!" Apparently, many other Americans felt the same way, and a growing movement of people who stated we were Taxed Enough Already started making themselves heard. The media mocked them, most of them not knowing or understanding our history as a nation. The initials for this movement spelled tea, a correlation to the Tea Party rebellion that led to our Revolution.

Things continued to get worse. To placate his supporters, Obama took over General Motors and offered a program called "Cash for Clunkers," a scheme to get cars into the hands of those who voted so he would "give them things," The cars that were traded in would have been suitable for many who couldn't afford a car, but the underlying message was the clunkers or old cars were bad for the environment, and the clunkers were demolished.

My friends had cars made in the USA by Saturn, but because Saturn was non-union, Saturn dealerships disappeared.

Scenes on television of people racing to a Wal Mart or other facility to get their "free" Obama cell phones and expedited food stamps while hard working Americans struggled to just make ends meet, fueled the movement even more.

The final straw? At least early in his presidency? Hillary's healthcare bill being pushed as Obamacare through a Health and Human services agency bloated with new hires and ideological puppets.

I personally recruited more than 5000 people to march on Washington to put an end to the madness. We had motorcades, busses, six or ten to a room and on September 12, 2009, more than a million people marched to the capitol to protest spending and Obamacare.

We could see Obama circling in his helicopter and hoped he realized the American people did not want this bill passed. Mainstream media reported that "thousands" had marched on Washington, many of them carrying Nazi signs. A lie. A lie to begin or further divide between blacks and whites. We were racist to demonstrate against a black president and racist to not support healthcare for the poor.

The most we accomplished was a delay in the passing of the bill, but maybe that was a good thing. Before Pelosi marched in with her giant gavel to declare victory, our efforts had slowed the

Obama agenda for several months, which gave people time to catch up with his real mission.

Then, in June, he went to Cairo, Egypt. His speech was the beginning of an apology tour that would enrage Americans and change the education of our children forever.

Not only did he lie about the Muslim influence and history in America, but he also, in the name of the American people, declared America's dedication to Islam. He announced a timeline for leaving Iraq, and a partnership with Hamas, a terrorist group, in Palestine.

His speech was long and I could see how his followers would be mesmerized, but I also knew many of his followers didn't understand a word he said, nor did they care.

Obama continued his apology tour, bowing to every Premier, Sheikh, President or head of state, and with each bow, I wanted nothing more than for him to be removed from office.

When he began running for his second term, the GOP did what it had now been doing for decades. They chose Mitt Romney, a Mormon, to run against Obama. The people had no choice.

The main differences between the two were taxes, Iraq and immigration, but Romney's religion kept many home. That, coupled with massive voter fraud, influenced by the mid- term losses of the House of Representatives, gave Obama his second term with a divided Congress.

That Thanksgiving, I wrote something to my followers on social media to try to keep them strong. We needed to take the Senate in two years to stop Obama from transforming America any more than it already was. Unemployment was up, food stamps were up, median income was down, and the deficit was nearly $17 trillion.

"It was just an idea. A land with spacious skies, majestic mountains, amber waves of grain, fruit trees, and oceans. People liked it here. People died trying to get here. People fought and died to stay here.

They arrived on ships, greeted by a native people who were curious, but friendly.

Some of the rich and elite scorned these people and thought their habits of honoring the sun and the moon, eating by hand, and dressing scantily, reduced them to savages. But most of the people who arrived on the shores came to be free. They escaped churches and religions and Kings and tyrants, and when they set foot in the new world, they knew they would forever call it home.

Oh, they had a lot to go through. The struggle of learning what to plant, when to do it, and how the weather would destroy it was new to most. This land had tornadoes and lightning, a strange phenomenon in many of their homelands, and earthquakes that would split the ground and ring newly hung barn bells miles away. In some places, the winters were colder than any had ever experienced, and in others, the summers were almost too hot to survive.

They built houses and churches, barns and bakeries, libraries and lumber mills. But the most important thing they built was history. Though many died younger than they should have from famine or disease or early wars, they told their stories to their children, and the children told them again to theirs. They spoke of pride in their work, their harvest, their good luck. They spoke of neighbors helping neighbors, raising children and barn walls. They spoke of hardship and the faith they maintained, their connection to God, and His help in all things.

They fought sometimes. After all, their differences were mighty and their histories diverse. It wasn't always easy to find likeminded people or those who would at least share their ideas. But they found ways, whether through barter or religion or common scars or horses, to maintain their love for their country, their community, and their family, to help to make it grow.

When King George II decided to exploit their happiness and good fortune through taxation, and never asked any of them if they wanted what he decreed, they remembered their ancestors and the meaning of freedom in a chosen land they called their own.

The wars were hard and the natives killed or displaced to make room for the influx of European thought and practice. Their language was garbled and many were often misunderstood, many others put to death for being different or from outside circles of popular thought.

A few men, and women, decided it was time to think about what constituted this land free of a King's power. They first declared their independence so no King of any country could enslave them again. That was a good first step, but they needed to define the constitution of the land and its people, a diverse population with varied backgrounds, religions and skills.

They said the land was united, through communities, though separate, and perhaps a set of uniting principles would help every town, every growing city, every single farmer or lumberjack, to have the inalienable right to life, liberty and the pursuit of happiness. What a grand and glorious idea.

They had written these rights into their declaration of freedom, and now they would be further defined, so that they may govern themselves and not be governed.

Boundaries were drawn and names given to just about every plot of land that could be claimed, with some held vacant for the common good. It was decided that all governing power should come from the bottom up, from the individual to his community, from the woman to her town, from the man to his state, and from each state to a central place of government. It should be, they said, a government of the people, by the people, and for the people.

And the people should and will have the right to determine how they will be governed. They will be able to speak without censorship and carry arms for protection, not only from each other, but mostly from the government. They should be able to assemble, peacefully, and within the limits of private property, and attend any church, practice any faith, without government interference. If they be housed, it will be by their labor and the friendly barter of neighbors. If they be educated, they will be given a reasonable time to learn the basics.

They covered as many rights as were suitable at the time and called it the Constitution of the United States of America. Without it, this new land could be corrupted and co-opted, overcome by tyrants, destroyed by the lawless and its people shackled to hand-outs, begging for food. Though some were not chosen to prosper or thrive as much as others, the people knew, from their history and religion and their beliefs, that they would do what they could to help those less fortunate. Charity began at home, and America was their home.

We've been through more wars since those times, and famines and tornadoes, hurricanes and blizzards. We've elected presidents and congresspeople, governors and mayors, all through the power of the ballot box and the constitutional rights afforded every legal citizen. We've known ancestors who came through Ellis Island, and sons who have traveled to faraway lands. During times of war, we've interred Italians, Japanese, Germans and anyone who posed a threat to our national freedom. We bought and sold slaves, be we black or white, and freed those enslaved, be they white or black. We have spent a little over 240 years learning how to be a self-governed, free and prosperous, constitutional-republic, the only one of its kind on a planet filled with hatred, bias and tyranny.

Have we now come full-circle? Are we still a free Republic? Does the Constitution still have its original intent?

We have a president who dishonors our flag, who has appointed a cabinet who wants America to become Europe. We have a president who makes congress irrelevant, and uses the power of the pen to enact and enforce laws that only he and his Muslim or Communist supporters believe in. We have resources being wasted, more poor than ever in our history, more simultaneous wars than ever before, and a prosperity that has been "spread around" to those who never believed in America, never helped a neighbor, never knelt in gratitude for the land of the free.

If we forget our history, we will repeat it. If we believe freedom is free, it will cost us our lives. If we open our borders, forget the boundaries of responsibility to a nation and its beliefs, we become a multi-colored ghetto waiting, not for God, but for the next hand-out, the next meal. If we choose to ignore or shred the documents that gave us, on our ancestor's blood, the knowledge of our few but important inalienable rights and the laws that keep us civil, we become nothing more than poor, angry and Godless people wandering the streets that once flourished, and waiting for the next free ride to tyranny.

Not the idea our founders had,
and not my idea of the United States of America.

So, I will stand with my ancestors, with my founding fathers and mothers. I will not let my country die or the freedoms we fought for become rewritten history. I stand ready, and when the bugle sounds with a million flags or 200 million flags, held tightly in the hands of those who know what freedom means, we will either fill the ballot boxes like the patriotic Americans and citizens we are, or we will lead the charge to remove the tyrants, secure our borders, restore our prosperity, and "spread the work around."

Unite now. That's the beginning of freedom. That's the call for unity. That's where our Constitution began. Believe in America. This is our beginning to restore the Republic, defeat Islam, eradicate Communism, and bring back our America as one nation, under God, indivisible, with liberty and justice for all."

CHAPTER 12

We have endured an Obama presidency, eight years of a war between Communism and Capitalism, Christianity and Islam Fundamentalism, white and black, the people, and the arrogant elite. No American who has fought to save the Republic should be ashamed or downtrodden. Many people gave up hours, days, weekends, and years to try to educate those who either couldn't or wouldn't grasp the severity of this failed President, the presidents before him or the agenda both he and congress forced us to accept. Obama has used his pen and his ideology to do exactly what he said he would do five days before his first election. He has fundamentally transformed the United States of America.

But we're not done.

We now have a choice between a proven corrupt politician, or a man even the GOP machine doesn't want in the Oval office,

We have a choice between more of Obama's policies which are really George Soros' policies, being enforced by Valerie Jarrett, or the policies of a man who didn't need to run for office, but forms his policies based on business acumen, international experience, and above all, honesty.

We have a choice to cower in silence while our votes are stolen, or to show up and be as sure as we can be, that the thieves don't strike as they have so often done before.

We have a choice between restoring an America with secure borders, good jobs, peace, and freedom, or an America overrun with migrants from countries that hate our freedom, our history, our very existence.

We have a choice, and it is this choice, this election, this year, and all years that follow that will determine if our children, our grandchildren, will ever have a choice again, will ever know what freedom is, will ever know what a glorious idea it was to form the greatest country in all history, in all the world, the United States of America.

-end-

www.ingramcontent.com/pod-product-compliance
Lightning Source LLC
Chambersburg PA
CBHW060308290526
45789CB00001B/447